Golden
Retrievers

SHEILA WEBSTER BONEHAM, Ph.D.

ANIMAL PLANET ♥ PET CARE LIBRARY

Golden Retrievers

Project Team
Editor: Stephanie Fornino
Copy Editor: Ellen Bingham
Interior Design: Leah Lococo Ltd. and Stephanie Krautheim
Design Layout: Tilly Grassa

T.F.H. Publications
President/CEO: Glen S. Axelrod
Executive Vice President: Mark E. Johnson
Publisher: Christopher T. Reggio
Production Manager: Kathy Bontz

T.F.H. Publications, Inc.
One TFH Plaza
Third and Union Avenues
Neptune City, NJ 07753

Discovery Communications, Inc. Book Development Team
Maureen Smith, Executive Vice President & General
  Manager, Animal Planet
Carol LeBlanc, Vice President, Marketing and Retail
  Development
Elizabeth Bakacs, Vice President, Creative Services
Peggy Ang, Director, Animal Planet Marketing
Caitlin Erb, Marketing Associate

Printed and bound in China

07 08 09 10   3 5 7 9 8 6 4 2
ISBN13 9-780793-83757-1
Library of Congress Cataloging-in-Publication Data

Boneham, Sheila Webster, 1952-
  Golden retrievers / Sheila Webster Boneham.
      p. cm. — (Animal Planet pet care library)
  Includes index.
  ISBN 0-7938-3757-X (alk. paper)
  1. Golden retriever. I. Animal Planet (Television network) II. Title. III. Series.
  SF429.G63B67 2006
  636.752'7—dc22   2006006197

This book has been published with the intent to provide accurate and authoritative information in regard to the subject matter within. While every precaution has been taken in preparation of this book, the author and publisher expressly disclaim responsibility for any errors, omissions, or adverse effects arising from the use or application of the information contained herein. The techniques and suggestions are used at the reader's discretion and are not to be considered a substitute for veterinary care. If you suspect a medical problem consult your veterinarian.

The Leader In Responsible Animal Care For Over 50 Years!™

www.tfh.com

CENTRAL
Garden & Pet

Table of Contents

Chapter 1

Why I Adore My Golden Retriever 5
Form Follows Function • A Golden Personality

Chapter 2

The Stuff of Everyday Life 13
Baby Gates • Bed • Collar • Crate • Exercise Pen • Food and Water
Bowls • Grooming Supplies • Identification • Leashes • Toys and Chewies

Chapter 3

Good Eating 23
What Your Golden Eats • Commercial Diets • Noncommercial Diets •
When and How to Feed Your Golden • Weighing In

Chapter 4

Looking Good 37
Brushing • Bathing • Foot and Nail Care • Ear Care • Eye Care •
Dental Care • Anal Sac Care

Chapter 5

Feeling Good 49
Finding a Golden Veterinarian • Altering Your Golden • Vaccinating
Against Disease • Parasites • Health Issues in Golden Retrievers •
First Aid • Alternative Therapies

Chapter 6

Being Good 71
What Is Dog Training, Anyway? • Training Tools • Socialization and
Growing Up • Crate Training • Housetraining • Basic Obedience Commands

Chapter 7

In the Doghouse 85
Barking • Chewing • Digging • Housetraining Problems • Jumping Up •
Nipping and Mouthing

Chapter 8

Stepping Out 95
Wherever You Go—Travel Tips • Competitive Activities for Goldens •
Noncompetitive Activities for Goldens

Resources 106
Index 109

Chapter 1

Why I Adore My
Golden Retriever

No sweeter or more beautiful dog walks the earth than the Golden Retriever, so it's no wonder these joyous, loving dogs consistently rank high among "most popular dog breeds." The Golden's physique and personality make him an outstanding companion in the right home, although he can be too big and too energetic for some people and situations. Let's look at the traits that endear the Golden to his many fans.

Form Follows Function

The Golden Retriever was developed in Scotland in the 19th century as a hunting companion for gamekeepers and gentlemen hunters. His primary job, retrieving shot birds from water and land, required the Golden to be a powerful, agile dog with energy to keep him going all day in the field, confidence to work away from his master, eagerness to keep him interested in his work, and a willingness to please his human partner. But, of course, even the most avid hunter doesn't hunt all the time, and the Golden Retriever also has the sweet, loving personality—amply reflected in his kind expression and joyful bearing—that makes him an unbeatable companion in the right environment.

The original Goldens' physical traits developed as breeders selected dogs whose form best enabled them to perform their work as hunting companions. Those same traits help the Golden Retriever of today to continue his traditional work and to be a canine athlete capable of excelling at competitive sports as well as all the activities expected of a beloved pet dog.

Height and Weight

Although not a giant, the Golden is a big dog. Ideally, a male Golden Retriever stands 23 to 24 inches (58.4 to 61.0 cm) tall at the withers (the highest point where the shoulder blades meet) and weighs 65 to 75 pounds (29.5 to 34.0 kg). A female stands 21½ to 22½ inches (54.6 to 57.2 cm) and weighs 55 to 65 pounds (25.0 to 29.5 kg).

Coat

The Golden Retriever takes his name from the glorious color of his coat, which the breed standard describes as "rich, lustrous golden of various shades."

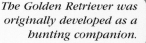

The Golden Retriever was originally developed as a hunting companion.

Although Goldens range in color from pale gold to deep reddish-bronze gold, extremely light or dark coats are considered undesirable. The feathers—long hair on the legs and tail—may be a lighter shade than the body, but no other color is allowed except for a few white hairs on the chest. As Goldens age, they show some graying on the face and body, but that shouldn't be confused with white markings present from puppyhood.

The Golden's double coat consists of an outercoat of long, water-repellent hair of medium texture over a dense undercoat of shorter hair. The outercoat may be straight or wavy and should lie close to the body. The hair on the throat, ruff (chest), underbody, back of the legs, and underside of the tail is long and thick, while the hair on the head, paws, and front of the legs is short. Stray hairs may be trimmed from the paws and around the ears, but otherwise the Golden's coat should be natural.

Head

The Golden Retriever should have a strong, broad skull with a well-defined, sloping stop (the point where the muzzle meets the skull, much like the bridge of your nose). The muzzle should be deep and wide, not pointy, and the length from the nose to the stop should be almost as long as the skull from the stop to the occiput (the bone that protrudes slightly at the back of the skull).

Who's Owned by a Golden Retriever?

It's no surprise that many famous people are owned by Golden Retrievers, including President Gerald Ford, whose Golden, Liberty, was said to be on call to jump on anyone who overstayed their welcome in the Oval Office. Authors J. A. Jance, Dean Koontz, and Sara Paretsky, Olympic figure-skating gold medalist Michelle Kwan, singers Jimmy Buffett and Enrique Iglesias, actors Betty White and Bill Murray, and many others have shared their lives with Golden Retrievers.

The Golden's eyes should express intelligence and friendliness and should be dark to medium brown surrounded by dark rims that fit snugly against the eyes. The Golden's silky ears should be set high behind the eyes and hang close to the dog's cheeks. If you pull your dog's ears forward, the tip of each ear should just cover the eye on that side. His nose should be black or brownish black, although it might fade to a lighter shade in cold weather.

The Golden's teeth should meet in a

scissors bite, which means that the outside edge of the lower incisors (front teeth) should just touch the inner edge of the upper incisors, and his jaws should be aligned evenly when you look from the front.

Body

The Golden Retriever's neck and back should appear sturdy and muscular without looking coarse. His back should be level horizontally to just above the hips and then slope slightly downward to the tail. His chest should be well developed, and the space between his front legs should be the width of a man's fist, including the thumb. His ribs should curve gently out and down from the spine, and he should have very little tuck-up (meaning that his belly shouldn't look "sucked up" like a Greyhound's does). The Golden's tail should be thick and muscular at the base and be carried level with the back. It may curve up slightly but should not be curled over the back or tucked between the legs. The tail should be well feathered, and the bones of the tail should reach to the point of the hock, the joint above the long bone of the lower leg. The Golden Retriever's legs should be strong, straight, and well muscled.

Gait

When the Golden trots, his movement should be free, strong, and coordinated. His legs should move in a straight line with his direction of movement, and as he increases his speed at a trot, the feet should converge toward a centerline of balance.

A Golden Personality

The Golden Retriever is no doubt best loved by his fans for his sparkling personality and solid temperament. Goldens of both sexes are friendly, reliable, confident, and affectionate toward people and other animals. Aggression, nervousness, and timidity are

The Golden Retriever takes his name from the glorious color of his coat.

completely abnormal in this wonderful breed. There is little difference in temperament between male and female Golden Retrievers; both are intelligent and loving, and both make excellent companions for adults and for children.

Ease of Housetraining

Goldens of both sexes housetrain easily if taught consistently (see Chapter 6), although some unneutered male Goldens will mark their territory with urine, especially if they've been used for breeding or if they detect other male dogs in the area. Some will also attempt to mount people and other dogs, an inappropriate behavior that can be embarrassing and potentially dangerous. Having your male Golden neutered will control both behaviors for the most part, especially if the surgery is performed before your dog reaches sexual maturity. Most breeders and vets recommend neutering at about six to nine months of age. Unspayed

SENIOR DOG TIP

When Is a Golden a Golden Oldie?

Every individual ages differently, but in general, your Golden Retriever will be considered a senior at around seven or eight years, and when he's around nine or ten, he'll show signs of real old age, possibly including gray hair on his face and body, clouding in his eyes, a bit less energy, and stiffness in his joints. The average life expectancy of a Golden Retriever is 10 to 12 years, and your older dog will need your love, attention, and daily care just as much as he did when younger.

females often mark territory as well, and they experience fertile heat periods twice a year and hormonal mood swings throughout their six-month cycles. Having your female spayed puts an end to messy heats, emotional ups and downs, and the risk of unwanted pregnancy.

Exercise Requirements

Goldens are designed to spend long hours working outdoors with hunters and therefore have abundant energy that has to be used up. Just how much exercise your individual Golden needs will depend on several factors, including his age, physical condition, and family lines (Goldens from field trial lines tend to be much more energetic than those from show lines, although there are exceptions). A healthy young Golden will need several active exercise sessions every day—aerobic walking, retrieving games, and swimming are all good ways to use up energy without putting too much stress on young joints and bones. Don't rely on your dog to exercise himself,

FAMILY-FRIENDLY TIP

Golden Retrievers and Kids

Golden Retrievers are among the best family dogs in the world. Although a Golden puppy or adolescent can be a bit too exuberant and overwhelm a small child or a feeble adult, Goldens are by nature kind, gentle, and loving dogs. With obedience training for manners and control, a Golden Retriever can be the ideal canine companion for playing ball, telling secrets to, and snuggling up with for children of all ages, as long as an adult takes ultimate responsibility for the dog's care.

though. Few dogs will self-exercise, and if you stick your Golden in the backyard by himself, he's more likely to stand and stare at the back door or take a nap than he is to run around.

Your Golden Retriever also requires mental exercise to develop properly and be as fine a companion as he can be. Training in basic obedience and in various sports and activities are good for the canine mind, as are games like "find the toy"

Much of the Golden's popularity is due to his solid temperament and sparkling personality.

and trick training. Boredom is one of the main causes of dog misbehavior, so finding a way to engage your Golden's mind will not only provide you with fun and entertainment but will head off many potential unwanted behaviors in your dog.

Environment

Although the Golden Retriever was bred to work in the great outdoors, he's not meant to live there. This kind, gentle dog thrives on human companionship and needs to live indoors as part of the family. Banishing a Golden to the backyard is not only unfair to your dog but will likely lead to nuisance behaviors born of loneliness and boredom. If your Golden lives indoors with you, the bond between you will become deeper and stronger, and your dog will do whatever you ask of him with enthusiasm and love.

Friendliness

Golden Retrievers are friendly to just about everyone and are not "one-person dogs." And although a Golden will probably defend someone he loves in a life-threatening situation, he is not by nature suspicious of strangers or protective, making him completely unsuited to any sort of guard work. On the contrary, most Golden owners expect that their dogs would offer burglars milk and cookies as well as the family silver.

11

Grooming Requirements

Goldens shed a little hair all the time and a lot in the spring and fall. Regular brushing at least once a week will help keep loose hair to a minimum and help prevent mats from forming in the long hair. To look his best, your Golden also needs to have the straggly hair trimmed from his ears, paws, and tail about once a month. See Chapter 4 for more information about grooming.

There are obviously many good reasons that the Golden Retriever is one of the world's most popular dogs. Although not the best breed for everyone, in the right home, this dog with the golden hair is indeed a treasure.

Why I Adore My Golden Retriever

The Stuff of
Everyday Life

Your Golden Retriever doesn't care about material possessions, but there are some supplies that will make life easier for you as a dog owner. Some of them will also keep your four-footed friend safer and healthier. Let's look at the basics.

Baby Gates

Baby gates—the sort that are tension-fitted into a doorway—are very useful for keeping your Golden in certain parts of the house. Standard baby gates, available from most discount, hardware, and baby stores, work fine in most cases, but many pet-supply catalogs offer special gates. Some are for wider openings, some fasten to the doorframe and swing open, some are extra tall, and so forth.

If you have a cat, a baby gate is a good way to block your dog's access to the cat's safe haven or food and litter box.

Bed

Dog beds come in a wide range of styles and prices, from thin pads to orthopedic foam to soft, loosely padded giant pillows. Most Goldens enjoy sacking out on a comfy bed, although most will also sleep soundly on the cold, hard floor, especially in hot weather. The main thing to consider when you choose a bed is size. Be sure that the bed is large enough to accommodate your Golden Retriever's body when he's stretched out and relaxed.

If you have a puppy or young dog who likes to chew and rip things up, wait until he outgrows this phase before you buy him a bed. And as your Golden ages, you may want to give him a bed with a bit more support for his old bones. Choose a bed with a

A crate can keep your Golden safe and out of trouble.

removable cover so that you can wash it, and if the bed has a soft filler, fluff it once in a while to redistribute particles that have clumped. Nobody likes a lumpy bed!

Collar

Your Golden needs at least one collar, and if you buy only one, make it a flat nylon or leather collar with a buckle or quick-release fastener. Check the fit often; you should be able to insert two fingers between the collar and your dog's neck. Readjust or replace the collar when necessary.

Crate

Whether you have a puppy or an adult, a crate can keep your Golden safe and out of trouble. Puppies aren't born knowing where to potty or what to play with. The same goes for adult dogs who haven't had the benefit of proper training. You have to keep your Golden safe when you can't supervise him, and you need to help him learn what you do and don't want him to do. But you can't supervise your Golden all the time, and that's where crates come in. Dogs are, by nature, den animals, and most of them like the safe, cozy environment that a crate provides.

Dog crates come in many styles and prices, so choose whatever will work best for you and your dog. An adult Golden will need a crate that's at least 24 inches (61.0 cm) wide by 36 inches

Set Up a Golden Care Schedule

If different members of your family participate in your Golden Retriever's care, post a "duty schedule" somewhere prominent so that everyone knows who's responsible for what. An erasable calendar works well for this, especially if you rotate duties. (That way, no one gets poop patrol all the time.) Include the time of day, each person's name, and the job (feed breakfast, feed dinner, brush, take out to potty, clean up yard, walk, train, and so on). Have everyone check off jobs as they finish them. A schedule reinforces the fact that your dog is a big responsibility and also ensures that he doesn't get two breakfasts and no walks.

(91.4 cm) long (a big Golden may need a bigger crate)—big enough for him to stand up, turn around, and lie down in comfortably. Be sure the door fits well and latches securely, so that your dog can't open it or poke a paw or his head through. You can put bedding in the

Dog Walkers and Doggy Daycare

If you have to be away from home for long hours, consider paying or bartering with a dog walker to exercise your Golden during the day. This is especially important while he's a puppy; you don't expect a baby to go all day without pottying, do you? Besides, your Golden will appreciate having a little company in the middle of a long day without you. If you hire a professional walker or pet sitter, be sure that she is insured and bonded against damages and that she's comfortable and competent handling a big dog. Check her references.

Doggy daycare is another option, but be cautious! Visit the facility during the times when your dog would be there. Check that the area is clean and free of hazards and that fresh water is always available. A responsible person should supervise all playtime. All dogs taken in for care should be required to have current vaccinations and veterinary records, including periodic fecal exams for parasites, and your own dog should be protected against fleas, heartworm, and other parasites prevalent where you live. Ask how possible aggression in playgroups is managed and what response plan is in place in case a dog is injured or becomes ill, or a man-made or natural emergency arises. A veterinarian should be on call, and reliable transportation should be available.

crate if your dog is housetrained and doesn't rip things up.

Exercise Pen

You might want to consider buying an exercise pen (x-pen), which is a pen made of segments that link together to form a small fenced-in area.

Traditional x-pens are made of eight heavy wire panels, each about 2 feet (0.6 m) wide. X-pens are also available in lighter-weight plastics and fabric. A Golden Retriever needs a pen that is at least 3 feet (0.9 m) tall.

The advantage of an x-pen is that it gives your dog more room than a crate to move around in but still keeps him safely confined when you can't supervise him. Even after puppyhood, an x-pen can be handy if your Golden is on restricted exercise due to illness or injury. There are disadvantages, though. For one thing, unless you anchor the pen, your Golden will be able to move it around. (A friend's Golden pup, Clancy, walked his x-pen more than 20 feet (6.1 m) across our training building to come see me one evening!) Many dogs also climb or jump out of x-pens or even lift them and crawl underneath, so this enclosure should never be trusted for confining your dog when you aren't nearby, especially outdoors.

Food and Water Bowls

You need bowls for food and water, but don't worry about different sizes for different ages. A Golden puppy can eat and drink from adult-size bowls.

You can find all sorts of dog bowls. Stainless steel bowls are sturdy, easy to clean, and resistant to chewing. Plastic bowls are lightweight and cheap, but cracks and scratches can harbor bacteria, and some dogs are allergic to plastic. Ceramic bowls are breakable, and some ceramics made outside of the United States contain lead and other toxins that can leach into food and water.

An exercise pen gives your dog more room to move around in than does a crate.

Licensing Your Golden

Most cities and many counties and states require that dogs be licensed. In some places, an unlicensed stray is euthanized quickly, so if your Golden gets lost, a license on his collar (along with ID and rabies tags) can help get him get back to you and may save his life.

the nail and a sharp blade that slides across the opening. A scissors-style clipper has two blades that cross in a scissors action, cutting the nail from both sides. Whichever kind you use, keep them sharp and in good working order. Poorly aligned or dull blades don't cut cleanly and may pinch. If you want to file the rough edges after clipping, an emery board made for acrylic nails works well on doggy nails. You can use a nail grinder to grind the nail rather than clipping it, but if you do, have a groomer or veterinarian

Grooming Supplies

You'll need some grooming supplies to keep your Golden glowing. (See Chapter 4.) For everyday grooming, you need a slicker brush, pin brush, shedding blade, and doggy dental products. If fleas or ticks are a problem, you'll want a flea comb and a tick remover, as well as an effective flea-control product. (See Chapter 5.)

Once every week or two, your Golden will need a nail trim. Doggy nail clippers come in two main types. The guillotine clipper has an opening into which you slip

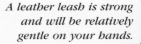

A leather leash is strong and will be relatively gentle on your hands.

show you how to use it properly.

Your Golden will probably need an occasional bath. There are all sorts of shampoos and other bath products available for dogs, but all you really need is a mild shampoo formulated for dogs. (Don't use people shampoos—they'll dry out your dog's skin and coat.) A cream rinse after bathing may reduce static electricity if it's a problem.

Identification

Your dog should carry identification in case he's ever lost—an ID tag with your phone number and his rabies and license tags should be attached to his collar. However, collars can be lost or removed, so consider a permanent form of identification as well.

Tattoos and microchips are commonly used for permanent identification. A microchip is a transmitter about the size of a grain of rice that is inserted by syringe under the skin over your dog's shoulders. It contains a number that is registered to your dog and that can be read by a special scanner. Your dog can also be tattooed on the belly or inside flank with an identifying number. For more information, check with your veterinarian.

Leashes

You need at least one leash. (A spare is a good idea.) Always leash your Golden when he's not inside walls or a

FAMILY-FRIENDLY TIP

Kids and Dog Care

Owning a dog can help a child learn about love and duty, but placing full responsibility for an animal's care into a child's hands is unfair to the child and to the dog and, frankly, is irresponsible on the part of the adult. Even the most dog-crazy child has other interests, and putting dog care in the way of other activities can cause the child to resent the dog—not your goal, I'm sure. Besides, your dog relies on people to guard his health and well-being, and children don't have the judgment and skills necessary to be fully responsible for another living creature.

fence—a ten-second squirrel chase into the street can end in tragedy, and even the best-trained dog can have a lapse in obedience.

A 4- to 6-foot (1.2 to 1.8 m) leather leash that's ½- to 1-inch (1.3 to 2.5 cm) wide is strong and relatively gentle on your hands. Nylon leashes are inexpensive, but some are abrasive and can burn or scrape your skin. Don't use a chain leash; it is ineffective for training and can injure you or your

19

Buy well-made chew toys, because they're safer and more durable than their less expensive counterparts.

dog. A retractable leash is nice for walks, allowing your dog a little more space while still keeping him safely tethered to you.

Toys and Chewies

Most Golden Retrievers are playful throughout their lives, so you'll want to buy some toys and some safe chewies. Goldens love to chase and fetch, and every Golden seems to have a favorite ball—just be sure that the balls you give your dog are too big for him to swallow. (A small ball caught on the fly can easily enter your dog's windpipe and suffocate him). Tennis balls are popular among the Golden set.

Most Goldens also like to chew, especially when they're young. Buy well-made chew toys; they're safer and longer lasting than cheap ones. Replace chew toys when they develop cracks or sharp points or edges or when they

SENIOR DOG TIP

Helping an Older Golden Adjust

Older adoptees usually settle into new homes fairly quickly, but there are some things you can do to make the transition smoother.

- If you already have a dog, make introductions on neutral ground where territory won't be an issue. Be ready to intervene, but let the dogs sniff one another. If they are friendly, take them home and let them continue to interact. If one or both are hostile to the other, keep their encounters short until they get used to one another.
- Don't leave your new dog loose with your old dog when you can't supervise them for the first few weeks. Separate them, or crate one or both.
- Crate your new dog or confine him to one room when you can't supervise him until you're confident that he's well-behaved and potty trained. Prevention works much better than correction.
- Spend lots of time with your new dog, and include him in your regular activities as much as possible. He'll quickly adopt you as his best friend. (Be sure your other dog also gets some private time with you, too!)
- Most Goldens get along with cats, but be cautious when bringing in an adult dog. Let your cat control all interactions, and teach your Golden not to chase the cat. Set up dog-free areas where your cat can sleep, eat, play, and use the litter box without canine "assistance," and be sure that the cat always has an escape route.

become too small to be safe. Dogs like furry toys and squeaky toys, but beware of plastic eyes, stuffing, and squeakers that can injure your dog if he swallows them. Dogs have individual preferences, so if your Golden doesn't like one chew toy, try another kind.

Your Golden Retriever won't care much about material possessions (except his gooey tennis ball or beat-up fuzzy toy), but having the right supplies and equipment to care for your dog can make life a lot easier for you.

Chapter 3

Good Eating

Your Golden Retriever is, to a great extent, what he eats. So how can you be sure his diet is healthful? First, learn about canine nutrition. Next, learn to judge how well your dog is doing on the diet he gets. Finally, keep in mind that many health problems can be linked to food—lack of energy, dry skin and coat, itchiness, "hot spots" (sores), and chronic diarrhea, among others. A change in diet may eliminate the source of a problem and prevent the need for drugs. So let's get started!

What Your Golden Eats

Your Golden Retriever is a carnivore. If he lived in the wild, he would kill and eat prey animals. His long canine teeth ("fangs") would be used to slash and hold his prey, and his sharp, serrated molars would shear off hunks of meat, which he would swallow with little chewing. He digests meat proteins efficiently. He probably enjoys fruits and veggies, but he gets few nutrients from them because his digestive system can't break down the cellulose walls of raw vegetable matter.

To stay healthy, your Golden needs to consume a balanced diet comprised of proteins, vitamins, carbohydrates, fats, minerals, and water. A high-quality canine diet provides all these nutrients in the right amounts to promote good health. If you feed your dog a high-quality dog food, you should not need to supplement his diet. In fact, oversupplementation with vitamins and minerals is a common source of health problems in dogs, especially in growing puppies, and can cause permanent damage to bones and tissues.

Commercial Diets

The number of dog foods on the market is astonishing, and they all claim to be the best, of course. So how can you choose the best food for your dog? What makes one food higher in quality than another? Ingredients! Many of the better dog foods use human-quality meats and other ingredients. They contain few, if any, fillers, chemicals, or dyes. They are nutritionally balanced and dense, which makes them more digestible, meaning that your dog uses more of the nutrients and produces smaller stools—a good thing with a dog the size of a Golden!

Most quality commercial foods are nutritionally balanced.

Inexpensive foods use low-quality ingredients, including less meat protein from low-quality sources, and contain more fat and fillers. Some are high in fat, which is cheaper than protein. Fat provides energy, so a dog on such a diet may seem to be getting proper nutrition, but the lack of protein, vitamins, and minerals in these foods will eventually damage his health as chronic malnutrition takes hold. The low-quality ingredients, chemical preservatives, and dyes found in some inexpensive foods have also been implicated in health and behavioral problems, including cancers, allergies, and hyperactivity.

Don't judge a food strictly by price, though. Some companies spend huge amounts for advertising campaigns, passing the cost on to the consumer. Some less-well-known brands have higher-quality ingredients and cost less than some of the well-known "premium" foods. In addition, high-quality foods cost more per pound (kg) than their lower-quality counterparts, but since you feed less per meal, the overall cost of a good food isn't necessarily more costly per meal. Besides, whatever money you save by buying a cheaper food will probably go to your veterinarian to treat health problems that might be avoided with better nutrition.

FAMILY-FRIENDLY TIP

Kids Feeding Dogs

Most kids like to help feed their dogs. Here are a few guidelines to help keep the process safe and sensible:

- Dogs don't always think that children outrank them in the family hierarchy, and a big dog can easily overwhelm a child who has desirable food. An adult should always be in a position to intervene, if necessary.
- Teach your dog to sit and wait politely until the child puts the food down.
- Teach your child to give your dog treats from an open palm.
- Teach your dog to allow people to take his food away.
- Teach your child not to take food away from your dog.
- Kids will happily overfeed your Golden into obesity or forget to feed him some meals, so an adult should supervise the feeding schedule and the amount of food served.

Dry Food (Kibble)

Dry food is less expensive than semi-moist and canned foods of equal quality. Kibble needs no refrigeration, although it should be stored in an

The Expert Knows

Supplements

If you feed your Golden Retriever a healthful, high-quality diet, he probably doesn't need dietary supplements. In fact, some supplements are dangerous. Too much calcium, for example, can cause serious, permanent damage to growing bones in puppies and may contribute to kidney stones and other problems in adult dogs. Hypervitaminosis (an excess of vitamins) is common in dogs who get supplements, and some vitamins, especially A and D, are toxic in large amounts. Don't give your Golden nutritional supplements unless your veterinarian advises you to do so.

airtight container and used by its expiration date. Dogs who eat kibble usually have cleaner teeth than dogs who eat wet food, because the dry bits scrape tartar from the teeth during chewing and don't cling to the teeth. Kibble-fed dogs also have firmer, smaller stools, especially if the food is high quality and therefore highly digestible.

Semi-Moist Food

Semi-moist dog foods are essentially soft kibble-like chunks. They usually cost more than kibble and produce larger, softer stools. They tend to stick

to teeth, harboring bacteria that cause gum disease, and most of them contain dyes and chemical preservatives that your dog just doesn't need.

Canned Food

Wet, or canned, foods cost more than equivalent-quality dry foods, because you're paying for the can and the water in the food. Canned foods may be recommended for a dog with certain dental or medical problems or for a dog whose appetite is poor due to illness or old age. However, a diet of canned food can cause tartar buildup, bad breath, flatulence, and large, soft, smelly stools. Canned food must be refrigerated once opened, and dishes must be washed after each meal to prevent spoilage and avoid attracting insects.

Special-Formula Food

Special-formula dog foods are available for dogs with special needs—puppies, seniors, active dogs, fat dogs, and dogs of particular sizes or even breeds. Most of these foods are just variations on the regular adult or maintenance version of the same food. Are these "special" foods better than a high-quality maintenance food? That's debatable. For instance, there is no scientific evidence that senior formulas improve the health or longevity of aging dogs. Many people overestimate their dogs' activity levels and feed high-calorie, high-protein "active dog" foods unnecessarily. As for puppy foods, many veterinarians and Golden breeders prefer high-quality adult food to keep growth rates slow and steady, because rapid growth can cause permanent damage to the skeletal system, especially in a large breed like the Golden Retriever. Reducing formulas may help get weight off quickly, but simply feeding a proper portion of regular food and providing adequate exercise is better for most dogs.

Some health problems, though, do warrant special-formula foods. If your dog is allergic to regular food (common food allergies include beef, poultry, corn, wheat, and soy), then a food that uses an alternative meat source (duck, fish, or venison, for example) or that replaces the commonly used grains with other vegetables (such as potatoes) may be a good choice. Special diets are also available, usually through a veterinarian, for dogs with specific health problems, such as kidney disease.

Noncommercial Diets

Some people prefer to feed their dogs homemade diets so that they can control the ingredients and provide more variety. I'm not talking about

Dogs who eat kibble usually have cleaner teeth than dogs who eat wet food.

Feeding Treats Wisely

Treats are great for training (see Chapter 6), but too many treats can turn your dog into a pudgy beggar. To avoid both results:

- Don't confuse treats with love; your dog doesn't need a cookie every ten minutes. He'll respond just as happily to an ear scratch, belly rub, ball game, or other token of your affection.
- Don't give your Golden treats just for breathing—have him respond to some command (*come, sit, lie down, roll over*) to earn the treat.
- Keep your dog's diet balanced and his total daily calories under control. For treats, use low-calories foods in very small amounts. (Some good choices are a portion of his daily kibble given one bit at a time, thinly sliced carrot or green bean, or tiny bits of nonfat string cheese.)

A well-planned homemade diet is fine for most dogs, but it poses some challenges. Your Golden's diet doesn't need to be completely balanced every day, but it does need to provide the proper balance of protein, carbohydrates, fats, essential fatty acids, minerals, and vitamins over the course of every few days. This is critical for a growing puppy, because poor nutrition during the growth phase—about 18 months for a Golden Retriever—can cause permanent damage to your dog's skeletal system and organs.

Home-Cooked Food

A wide variety of meats (beef, poultry, lamb, venison, and fish), vegetables, fruits (no grapes or raisins), grains, and dairy products can be included in a cooked canine diet. Some people cook a large batch of food and freeze it in serving-size containers, which can be thawed for individual meals. Others prefer to cook meals fresh each time.

If you want to cook for your dog, learn as much as you can about canine nutrition from reliable sources. A complete discussion of the subject is beyond the scope of this book, but a number of good (and bad—be careful!) books and websites are available on the subject.

Raw Food

One variation on the homemade diet is the raw-food diet, commonly known as

table scraps and leftovers but a carefully planned and prepared diet of high-quality meats, poultry, fish, eggs, dairy products, cooked vegetables, and possibly grains.

the B.A.R.F. diet, which stands for Bones and Raw Food or Biologically Appropriate Raw Food. There are many variations on the B.A.R.F. diet, but most "BARFers" feed their dogs raw chicken and turkey bones, adding organ meat (liver, kidney, heart, brain, tongue, and tripe) and eggs from time to time. They also include green leafy vegetables, usually after running them though a food processor or juicer, and various combinations of vegetable oils, brewer's yeast, kelp, apple cider vinegar, fresh and dried fruits, and/or raw honey. Some add small helpings of grains and dairy products, particularly raw goat milk, cottage cheese, and plain yogurt.

Homemade diets, especially the raw-food diet, require a lot of planning, preparation time, and storage space. In addition, it's essential to handle raw meat very carefully. Raw meats, poultry in particular, contain bacteria that can cause food poisoning and can contain parasites and their eggs and larva. To protect yourself and your family, it's essential to keep all utensils and work spaces scrupulously clean and to wash your hands with soap and water after handling raw meat.

Your dog should have access to clean, fresh water at all times.

When and How to Feed Your Golden

Everyone seems to have an opinion about how often and when to feed dogs. The best feeding schedule is the one that works for your dog and for you. Here are some things to consider as you plan your dog's mealtimes.

Feeding Chart

	Puppies (7 weeks to 4–6 months)	Adolescents (4–6 months to 18–24 months)	Active Adults (2 to 7+ years)	Sedentary Adults (2 to 7+ years)	Seniors (7 years and older)
Times per Day	3	2–3	1–2	1–2	2–3
Best Food	Adult maintenance diet or puppy formula until 4–6 months	Adult maintenance diet	Adult maintenance diet; high-performance diet only in case of true working dogs	Adult maintenance diet in moderation; low-calorie adult food in some cases	Adult maintenance diet; senior formula, if desired

Feeding Schedules

Many people think that dogs who have access to food at all times won't get fat. Not true! "Free-fed" dogs often become obese. Scheduled feeding, on the other hand, gives you control over your dog's food intake and therefore his weight. Scheduled feeding also makes it easier to monitor your dog's health. Lack of appetite is often the first sign of illness, and if you free feed, you may not notice right away if he stops eating.

Free feeding also makes housetraining more difficult, because a random eating schedule leads to random potty breaks, whereas scheduled meals make for more regular elimination. If you use treats to motivate and reward your dog when training, he'll be more interested in them if he doesn't have free access to food. If you travel with your dog, free feeding is impractical, and if you board him when you're away, he'll be fed on a schedule, adding more stress to the experience.

Water is a different matter. Your dog should have free access to clean, fresh water. The only times water should be limited are at night while housetraining a puppy, before anesthesia, and as advised by your veterinarian.

other signs of an insufficient diet, talk to your vet. Your dog may benefit from a food with higher caloric density.

If your senior Golden is healthy but loses interest in his food, try warming it a bit to make it more fragrant. A little warm water or unsalted broth over dry kibble works well, or try a few seconds in a microwave for soft foods, although you must be careful not to make the food too hot. You could also add a spoonful of cottage cheese, plain yogurt, or high-quality canned dog food to your dog's dry food—just watch the calories. Some elderly dogs also do better when their daily ration is split into three mealtimes a day.

If your dog stops eating at any age, consult your vet, because loss of appetite or unexplained weight loss can indicate a serious health problem. Dehydration is also a problem with some elderly dogs. If your Golden is ill or has trouble getting around, he may not drink enough. Be sure that he has easy access to water by putting several bowls around the house and yard.

Feeding the Senior Golden

There's quite a bit of controversy about how best to feed senior dogs. Large dogs like Golden Retrievers are generally considered to be "seniors" beginning at about seven years of age, but of course individual animals age differently. If your Golden is healthy and in good condition, he probably doesn't need any change in his diet. Some elderly dogs, however, have trouble digesting their food efficiently and can suffer from malnutrition even when eating a high-quality food. If your older Golden is losing weight or showing

Feeding Guidelines

The best number of meals and the times to feed them depend in part on your schedule and in part on your Golden's age. There's no single "correct" approach to feeding. Still, some general guidelines do apply to feeding dogs at different stages in their lives.

Young puppies need to eat more frequently than older puppies and adults do, because their stomachs are too small to hold all the food they need in a day in just one or two feedings. Most breeders recommend three meals a day for a Golden Retriever puppy who is 7 to 16 weeks old. If possible, space the meals evenly during your waking hours, giving your puppy a morning meal, a noon or afternoon meal, and an evening meal. Allow at least a couple hours between the last meal and bedtime, so that your puppy will eliminate before he goes to bed for the night. When he's about 16 weeks old, you can switch your puppy to two meals a day if you prefer. Puppies tend to eliminate shortly after they eat, so feeding your puppy on a regular schedule will help with potty training. When your pup is older and reliably housetrained, his feeding schedule doesn't need to be quite so rigid.

During adolescence—from about 6 to 18 months—your Golden puppy should eat two meals a day. If his food is fulfilling his nutritional needs, he will show good bone and muscle development and be neither skinny nor fat. He should be active and alert, and his coat should have a healthy shine.

As your Golden stops growing and matures into adulthood, he'll need fewer calories per day, even if he's active. Adult Goldens need to eat once or twice a day. I prefer twice-a-day feedings, but many dogs do fine on one meal a day. Either way, his total daily allotment should be the same.

Weighing In

Most Golden Retrievers love to eat, and most people enjoy making their dogs happy, which is easy to do with yummy handouts. Unfortunately, obesity contributes to serious health problems, including heart disease, diabetes, pancreatitis, respiratory problems, orthopedic problems, and arthritis. If your Golden is overweight, he won't be able to run as fast or jump as high without hurting himself, he'll overheat more easily, and he'll tire more quickly. He may develop weight-related health problems and will probably die younger than he would if you kept the weight off him.

Ideally, your Golden will weigh the proper amount from puppyhood through old age, but extra pounds (kg) can sneak on before you realize it. Healthy Goldens weigh anywhere from 50 to 80 pounds (22.7 to 36.3 kg), so it's essential to remember that proper weight is highly individual. The healthiest weight for your dog will depend on his height, bone structure (light, medium, or heavy bone), and condition (muscle weighs more than fat).

Weighing your dog at regular intervals will tell you whether he's gaining or losing weight, but it won't tell you whether that weight is proper for promoting his good health. Many veterinarians are so accustomed to seeing overweight dogs that they don't always alert their clients to excess weight in their pets, so you need to learn to do that yourself.

Is Your Golden Overweight?

To assess whether your Golden's weight is appropriate, you need to use your hands and your eyes. First, straddle your dog's spine with your thumb on one side and index finger on the other. Start at the shoulders, and move your fingers along his spine toward his tail. You should easily feel the ribs that are attached to the vertebrae without pushing down hard. Then look down on your dog's back when he's standing. You should see a distinct "waist" behind his ribs; that is, a narrowing of his body between the ribs and hips. If you can't feel ribs or see a waist, your dog needs to lose weight.

If you're consistent about not feeding your dog from the table, he won't beg while you're trying to eat.

How to Take Off the Excess Weight

Don't panic—it is possible to take weight off a pudgy pooch. Here are some tips for doggy dieters:

• Use the recommended servings on dog food containers only as rough starting points—they are usually more food than the average dog needs.

• Reduce the amount of food your overweight dog receives. If you want to make him feel more full on less dry food, soak half of his kibble in water for a half hour or so; the pieces will expand and be more filling. At mealtime, mix a half-portion of dry food with the soaked food and serve. Another way to add bulk with fewer calories is to cut back on dog food and add a low-calorie, high-fiber food to his meal: unsalted green beans (uncooked fresh beans are fine), lettuce or spinach, canned pumpkin (not pie filling, just pumpkin), or unsalted, air-popped popcorn (unless he's allergic to corn).

- Ask your vet about a weight-loss or lower-calorie food, but use caution. I know lots of overweight dogs who have been on "light" food for years. Too much food makes for a fat dog.

- Measure your dog's food with a standard measuring cup. It's easy to scoop up "one serving" that's closer to two.

- Control the number of treats your dog gets during the day, and be sure other members of your household don't give him extras. One approach is to put each day's allotment in a container so that you don't give more than you think you're giving. You can also set aside part of your dog's daily portions to use as treats; a single piece of kibble delights most dogs.

Adjust your dog's diet as necessary to keep him at an appropriate weight. He'll live a longer, healthier, happier life and look a lot better, too.

Your Golden Retriever's diet doesn't have to be fancy, but it should be made of the right amount of high-quality nutrients to promote lifelong

Training Your Golden Not to Beg

If you want your Golden Retriever to stare at you and your guests and slobber and whine whenever you have something to eat, you can easily train him to beg. All you have to do is give in once to those big, brown, hopeful, hungry eyes. But if you want your dog to lie down quietly while you eat, don't reward him for begging—ever! If you give in even once, he'll be much more persistent the next time. Teach him to lie down and mind his own business when you or anyone else is eating, whether at the dinner table or in front of the television. If you're consistent about not rewarding your dog for begging, he won't engage in that behavior.

good health. You can ensure that your dog's diet suits him by knowing what's in his food and by learning to assess his weight and physical condition. He'll thank you for your dietary attention with better health and behavior and a Golden glow to match.

Chapter 4

Looking Good

Regular grooming will help keep your Golden
Retriever looking and feeling his best. It will also
alert you to cuts, bumps, sore spots, and other early
signs of health problems and provide some quality
time for you and your dog to interact quietly.

Try to see grooming not as a chore but as a special activity you share with your dog. In fact, grooming sessions should be pleasant for both of you. If you treat him gently and talk to him as you groom him, your Golden will learn to trust your hands and enjoy the way they feel on his body, just as you enjoy the feel of his fur against your skin. Infrequent marathon grooming sessions can be stressful for both you and your dog, so try to schedule frequent, short sessions so that you can both relax and enjoy your time together.

Brushing

Regular brushing once or twice a week will help keep your Golden's coat clean, glowing, and free of tangles. It will also stimulate circulation and help keep his skin in good condition. There are housekeeping benefits, too—a well-brushed coat sheds less, making for less hair left behind on carpets and upholstery.

How to Brush Your Golden

Before you brush, lightly spritz your dog's coat with water or a dilute conditioner—1 tablespoon (14.8 ml) conditioner in 16 ounces (473.2 ml) of water—to reduce static and prevent breakage. Then brush or comb his hair in the direction the coat grows. On areas where the hair is longer (his tail, behind his ears, and the back of his legs and rear end), divide the hair into sections and brush or comb each separately, and then smooth the sections together. Be sure to brush hair all the way down to the skin to prevent matting, but don't push hard against the skin, especially with sharp metal brushes that can scratch.

Grooming Supplies for Golden Glow

Just a few basic grooming supplies will keep your Golden Retriever looking his best.

- cream rinse formulated for dogs (optional)
- doggy toothpaste and toothbrush
- ear cleaner
- file or nail grinder for smoothing nails (optional)
- flea comb
- nail clippers
- pin brush for long hair
- regular comb for the shorter hair on the head and legs (optional)
- shampoo formulated for dogs
- slicker brush for smoothing the coat

Bathing

Most Golden Retrievers love the water, but that doesn't mean they love bath time. However, if you take the time to teach your dog that baths aren't so bad, you'll find that the whole process will be a lot more pleasant for both of you.

How to Bathe Your Golden

Start teaching your Golden to enjoy the tub before he needs a bath. Like all training, this "prebath training" takes a little time and planning, but it teaches your dog to accept baths without fear and resistance. To begin, put him into the tub, give him a treat while you praise him, and then if he's quiet, let him get out. If he struggles, hold him firmly but gently in the tub and talk to him quietly. When he stops struggling, give him another treat, and take him out of the tub. Don't praise or reward him when he gets out—you want him to understand that being in the tub, not getting out, is good. Repeat this game once or twice a day for a few days, having your dog stay in the tub a little longer each time. When he's comfortable in the dry tub, add a little lukewarm water so that he gets his feet wet. When he's comfortable with getting his feet wet, begin to wet his body with lukewarm water from a sprayer or by pouring water onto him

Regular brushing once or twice a week will keep your Golden's coat in beautiful condition.

39

Looking Good

from an unbreakable container. Reward and praise him while you wet him. When he accepts that calmly, he's ready for a real bath.

Assemble all your bath supplies before you start bathing your Golden. You don't want to discover that you've forgotten something when your dog is wet and soapy! Here's what you need:

- brush
- cotton balls
- hose or unbreakable container for rinsing
- mild shampoo formulated for dogs
- nonslip mat
- one or two towels
- ophthalmic ointment

Before you wet your Golden, brush him to remove loose hair and foreign matter. Insert a cotton ball gently into the opening of each ear to protect the

The Expert Knows

Grooming as a Health Check

Grooming sessions are perfect times for checking your Golden for early signs of medical problems. Be alert for:
• bumps, cuts, sores, or sensitive areas on your dog's body
• cuts, lumps, bleeding, or a bad odor in his mouth
• excessive discharge, tenderness, redness, or a bad odor from his ears
• irritation in or around his eyes
• signs of parasites or other skin problems
See your vet before a small problem becomes a big one.

can make lathering and rinsing easier (and save money) by diluting your dog's shampoo before you apply it. (Mix one part shampoo with one or two parts water.)

If your dog has fleas, you can kill them with a regular dog shampoo. Begin with a "collar" of lather high on your dog's neck to keep any fleas that try to leave his body from hiding in his ears, and then lather the rest of his body. Leave the lather on for about ten minutes to drown the fleas, and then rinse. While you're waiting, check his ears and head for fleas, remove them by hand or with a flea comb, and drop them into a container of soapy water.

Next, rinse your dog thoroughly, because soap residue can cause skin irritation. Soap tends to hide in the armpits, under the hind legs, and in the groove along the underside between the ribs, so check those areas carefully. When all the soap is out, gently squeeze the excess water from your dog's coat with your hands. Then pat him all over with a towel, squeezing the long hair on his chest, belly, and legs with the towel. Don't rub—you'll create tangles. Wet dogs like to run and roll and rub on things (carpets, walls, furniture, bedspreads), so put a collar and leash on your dog before you let him go.

If you blow your Golden's coat dry,

ear canal against water. Soap can burn your dog's eyes, so apply an ophthalmic ointment (available from your vet, groomer, or pet supply store) to the eyes, or be *very careful* not to get soap into his eyes. Now put your dog into the tub, and don't forget to praise and reward him.

Using cool to lukewarm water, wet your dog thoroughly, and then apply shampoo and work it in with your fingers, beginning at your dog's neck and working toward the tail. Be sure to wash his belly, under his back legs, and under his tail. Use a washcloth on his face to avoid getting shampoo in his eyes. You use a cool setting. Hot air will damage his skin and coat and in warm weather can overheat your dog. If you let your dog air-dry, confine him to a "waterproof" room or to his crate until he's dry. Keep him warm and out of drafts. He may need to potty after his bath; take him on a leash, or you may find your clean Golden rolling around in the dirt.

Foot and Nail Care

Golden Retrievers have such beautiful, big, strong feet that it's easy to forget they need care to stay that way. But consider how much wear and tear you put on your shoes, and then transfer that thought to your dog's paws. If your Golden spends much time outdoors, it's even more important to help him keep his feet healthy.

How to Care for Your Golden's Feet and Nails

The long hair between your Golden's foot pads can reduce his traction on smooth surfaces and collect burrs, small stones, ice balls, and other debris, so check his feet often and keep them trimmed.

Overgrown nails can prevent your dog's foot from making proper contact with the ground, potentially distorting his foot permanently and making it painful for him to walk. If you can hear your Golden's nails clicking when

he walks, they're too long.

Prepare your dog for pedicures before you start clipping. When you're relaxing together, handle his feet one at a time, gently massaging and flexing his toes. This simple preparation teaches your dog that having his feet handled isn't unpleasant. In fact, many dogs love a nice foot massage. Do this during several daily sessions.

When your dog accepts having his feet held, begin trimming. If he still struggles when you clip, trim just one nail, give him a treat, and then release his paw. Handle his other paws, one at a time, without clipping, and then quit for a while. Continue to play with his feet between trimming sessions. Soon you'll be able to trim all his nails in one stress-free session.

When you trim nails, both you and

When bathing your dog, use a shampoo that is specially formulated for dogs.

Grooming Table

A grooming table made for dogs can be a handy tool for grooming your Golden. It puts your dog within easy reach so that you can groom him without bending over. Many dogs stand still better when they're up off the ground, once they get used to the table. You can purchase a folding, portable grooming table from most pet supply stores, or you can use a sturdy table. For your dog's safety:

- Use a table that is sturdy enough to hold a big dog.
- Provide a nonslip, easy-to-clean surface for your dog to stand on.
- Tie your dog or have someone hold him if you can't rely on him to stay. (Commercial tables have arm-and-noose arrangements for that purpose.)
- Never leave your dog on a grooming table unsupervised— he could be seriously injured if he jumps or falls off.

your dog need to be comfortable, and you need good light for the job. You can trim nails with your dog standing, sitting, or lying down; just be sure that he'll stay put. If necessary, tie him to something secure, or have someone hold him. Hold your dog's paw firmly but gently. Press the bottom of the footpad lightly to extend the nails. Trim the tip of each nail below the spot where the nail narrows and curves downward. Now look at the end of the nail; if you see a black dot near the center, that's the quick (the living part of the nail), and you've trimmed enough. If not, carefully trim a little more. Trim all your dog's nails, front and back, and don't forget the dewclaws, those little nails on the inside of the legs. If the newly clipped nails have sharp, rough edges, you can smooth

After shampooing your dog, be sure to rinse thoroughly, as soap residue can cause skin irritation.

them with strokes of an emery board.

If you accidentally cut into the quick, the nail may bleed. Cornstarch or styptic powder (available from pet supply or drug stores) will stop the bleeding. Just put a little of it into a shallow dish or the palm of your hand, and dip the nail into it.

If you're nervous about nail trimming, have your veterinarian show you the proper angle, length, and technique. As a last resort, have your Golden's nails trimmed at the vet's office or by a groomer. Don't wait for your dog's annual exam, though. His nails should be trimmed every three to six weeks, depending on how quickly they grow and how much they are worn down on rough surfaces.

Ear Care

Those beautiful, silky Golden ears are, unfortunately, prone to problems, in part because the ear leather (or flap) lies close to the head, holding moisture in the ear canal and creating ideal living quarters for yeast or bacteria, which may grow out of control due to allergies, hormonal problems, and/or excess moisture introduced when the dog swims or gets a bath. Ear mites, small arthropods related to spiders and ticks, are more common in cats than in dogs, but if your Golden has mites and is allergic to their saliva, even a few will make his ears unbearably itchy. And a rambunctious Golden can easily get plant matter, dirt, or other things in

FAMILY-FRIENDLY TIP

Kids and Dog Grooming

Most kids love to brush dogs, and they can learn a lot about the importance of personal hygiene by helping with your Golden's grooming. Which grooming tasks a child can undertake will depend on her age and ability. Brushing is relatively easy for younger children, and kids can help with baths. More delicate tasks, though, such as ear cleaning, toothbrushing, and nail trimming are more suited to an adult or to an older child under adult supervision. Don't leave all grooming responsibilities to a child; an adult needs to supervise to be sure grooming is gentle and thorough.

his ear, any of which can cause irritation or injury.

How to Care for Your Golden's Ears

Check your Golden's ears at least once a week. The skin inside his ears should be clean and pink or flesh colored, not dirty, red, or inflamed. A little wax is normal, but a lot of dirty-looking discharge is not. There shouldn't be any strong or objectionable odor coming from the ears.

If you see or smell anything

Your Golden's nails should be trimmed every three to six weeks, depending on how quickly they grow and how much they are worn down.

Ear cleaning can get messy, so before you begin, take your Golden outdoors or to a room where flying cleaner and wax won't be a problem. Squirt the cleaner into the ear, and then cover the opening with the ear flap and massage for a few seconds. When you let go, your dog will shake to clear his ears, so stand back! When he's finished, wipe his ears gently with a cotton ball or tissue.

Eye Care

There's nothing sweeter than the loving look in a Golden Retriever's eyes, and there are some things you can do to keep your dog's eyes healthy and glowing.

How to Care for Your Golden's Eyes

Routine eye care is simple. First, protect your dog's eyes from injury in risky situations. Soap and chemicals can seriously damage delicate eye tissues, so be careful when bathing your dog or applying insect repellents or other chemicals to his coat. When your Golden rides in a vehicle, don't let him hang his head out the window; the momentary pleasure isn't worth the risk of permanent injury from a fast-flying bug or bit of dirt.

It's normal for your dog to collect some mucus at the inner corners of his eyes, but built-up "eye gunk" is an ideal

abnormal, if your dog repeatedly scratches or rubs his ears or head, if he often shakes or tilts his head, or if his ears are sensitive, he may have a problem. Ear infections are painful and can be difficult to cure, and they can lead to permanent hearing loss. Accurate diagnosis is critical to effective treatment, and applying the wrong over-the-counter or homemade remedy will prolong the problem and may cause more damage.

If your Golden's ears are not inflamed or sensitive, and you don't see him scratching at them, you can clean them with a commercial or homemade ear cleaner. If they seem very waxy, or if he plays in water frequently, clean his ears about once a week with a cleaner designed to keep the ear canal free of excess moisture, yeast, and bacteria.

breeding ground for bacteria that can cause an eye infection, so gently wipe the mucus away with a moist washcloth or tissue once or twice a day.

Redness, swelling, excess tearing or mucus, or squinting may indicate an eye infection, abrasion, or other problem. Don't delay a trip to the vet if you see any of these symptoms—quick treatment may prevent a long-term problem and permanent injury.

Older dogs often develop a cloudiness known as *nuclear sclerosis* on the lens of the eye. It usually does not affect vision. However, a cloudy appearance may also be caused by a cataract, which can impair vision or even cause blindness. If you see changes in your older Golden's eyes, ask your vet to take a look.

Dental Care

Cavities are rare in dogs who eat normal canine diets free of sugary goodies. Gum disease, on the other hand, is common in adult dogs, because food particles that remain caught along the gum line harbor bacteria that form *plaque*. If not removed, the plaque turns to *tartar* (calculus), a hard deposit that irritates the gums, causing *gingivitis* (inflammation of the gums) and *periodontal disease,* characterized by abscesses, infection, and tooth and bone loss. The bacteria can also enter the bloodstream and travel throughout the body, contributing to heart, liver, and kidney disease. Luckily, you can protect

No Smelly Dogs or Doggy Breath

A healthy Golden Retriever is not a smelly dog. If you notice an unpleasant odor coming from your dog, and he hasn't rolled in something yucky, follow your nose, see your vet, and fix the problem, which may be caused by one or more of the following factors:

• broken or decayed tooth, or gum disease
• ear infection
• infected or impacted anal glands
• intestinal or stomach gas
• oil, bacteria, yeast, or foreign substance on the skin or coat

your Golden from gum disease by following a simple dental care routine consisting of home care and periodic checkups and cleaning by your vet.

How to Care for Your Golden's Teeth

Ideally, you should brush your Golden's teeth every day to remove plaque. Realistically, brushing every two or three days will help prevent tartar from forming and will also alert you quickly

Regular dental examinations are an integral part of your Golden puppy's grooming and healthcare routine.

veterinary care and a thorough cleaning under anesthesia about once a year. If he develops bad breath, visible tartar, bleeding gums, or other oral problems between regular examinations, see your vet.

In addition to brushing your dog's teeth regularly, you can slow the formation of dental plaque by feeding your Golden a high-quality dry dog food. Dogs also clean their teeth by chewing appropriate chewies and dental devices or raw or sterilized beef bones.

If you have a Golden Retriever puppy, check his mouth and teeth every few days. Like human babies, puppies are born without teeth. Their *deciduous,* or baby, teeth come in at about four weeks and are replaced by permanent teeth between three and five months. Sometimes a baby tooth is *retained* when the permanent tooth doesn't push it out completely. Retained deciduous teeth, most often incisors or upper canines ("fangs"), will cause the permanent teeth to be misaligned and will keep the jaw bones from developing properly, leading to pain, difficulty eating, and other problems. If you think your Golden puppy has retained a baby tooth, see your vet.

Anal Sac Care

Like other predators, your Golden has a distinctive odor that identifies him to

to any injuries, broken teeth, or other problems in his mouth. Be sure to use dental care products made for dogs; toothpaste made for people can make your dog sick if he swallows it, and toothbrushes for dogs are smaller, softer, and differently shaped from ours. You may find that you prefer a dental sponge, a small disposable sponge with a flexible handle, or a finger brush that fits over your finger, instead of a regular toothbrush. Ask your vet about toothbrushes, plaque removers, and toothpastes, and ask her to show you how to use them properly. If you make doggy toothbrushing just a normal part of your daily routine, you'll find that the few minutes you invest will make a big difference in your dog's oral health.

Your Golden should have periodic dental checkups as part of his regular other dogs. This odor is produced by *anal sacs* (anal glands) located on both sides and slightly below his anus. It's the odor from the anal sacs that dogs are checking when they greet each other with a friendly fanny sniff.

In a healthy dog, the anal glands *express,* or empty, their fluid with every bowel movement. That's why dogs find poop so fascinating—each one is a sign that says, "I was here." Sometimes the anal glands don't empty themselves normally, though, and if too much fluid is retained, the glands can become impacted. Although impacted glands are not dangerous, they are uncomfortable. To get some relief, the dog may bite at the area or scoot his rear end along the ground, possibly damaging the delicate tissue around his anus. Impacted anal glands can also make bowel movements difficult or painful and can develop into painful infections or abscesses. Most Goldens who are fed good-quality food don't have anal gland problems, but it's good to recognize the symptoms just in case.

How to Care for Your Golden's Anal Sacs

Impacted anal glands can often be relieved by manually expressing, or squeezing out, the fluid. If you're so inclined, you can have your vet or groomer teach you how to express your dog's glands if they need it. If that's not a skill you want to add to your repertoire, have your vet or groomer do

SENIOR DOG TIP

Grooming the Older Golden

Don't neglect to groom your senior Golden; he needs good, regular care even more in his golden years. Be gentle, especially if your dog has arthritis or other health problems, and keep sessions short so that he doesn't become exhausted. Be alert to lumps and bumps, sensitive areas, dental problems, and changes in his ears, eyes, and skin. And be sure to give him lots of smooches. Enjoy the special love and dignity that comes to the aging canine.

the job if and when necessary.

Dogs with chronically impacted anal glands sometimes benefit from a high-fiber diet, which creates bulkier stools that empty the glands when they pass. In severe cases, the anal glands can be removed.

The benefits of good grooming more than compensate for the relatively little time and effort required. Your house will stay cleaner, and your dog will be healthier and happier. He'll look his beautiful, Golden best, which can't help but make you smile.

Looking Good

Chapter 5

Feeling Good

Your Golden Retriever will live a longer, healthier life if you provide him with good veterinary care and take steps to safeguard his health. In this chapter, we will go over the basics of good preventive health care.

Finding a Golden Veterinarian

You will entrust your dog's health—in fact, his life—to your veterinarian, and you'll spend significant money on vet care over the years, so ask breeders, rescuers, your obedience instructor, members of local dog clubs, and your friends who have dogs what they like about their vets and whether there's anyone in the area they avoid, and why. If you try a vet but don't care for her or her clinic, look for another. Don't settle for a vet you don't like or trust. Your vet should show a genuine interest in your dog and in your concerns and should be willing and able to clearly answer your questions and discuss options.

Your Golden should have a complete examination at least once a year, during which your vet will check your Golden's general health and condition, compare his current condition against previous records, and note any important changes. She'll listen to your dog's heart and lungs, check his joints for range of motion and signs of discomfort, and examine his skin and coat, ears, gums, bite, and external eye area. If you live where heartworm is a problem, your vet will draw blood to check for

heartworm larvae, and she'll want to check a fecal sample to be sure your dog has no intestinal parasites. Depending on your Golden's age and health status, your vet may recommend blood work to check for a variety of potential problems. If you've noticed anything that may relate to your dog's health, be sure to tell your vet.

Altering Your Golden

Responsible dog ownership includes a commitment to the lifelong welfare of any puppies your Golden produces, so keeping your pet sexually intact is a big commitment. However, you don't have

Your Golden should have a complete physical examination at least once a year.

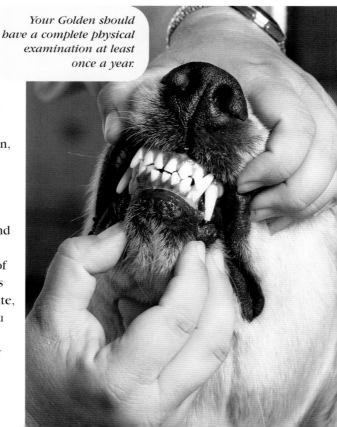

to worry about this if you alter your Golden (*spay* or *castrate*). Besides, altering benefits your dog's physical and emotional health—and altered dogs live longer.

Spaying (removal of the ovaries and uterus) prevents pregnancy and life-threatening cancers of the uterus, ovaries, and breasts, as well as the constant hormonal shifts and twice-yearly heat cycles that can make an unspayed female a challenge to live with.

Castration prevents testicular cancer, lowers the risk of prostate problems, and minimizes annoying stud-dog behaviors, including territorial urine marking, roaming in search of females in heat, and obsessive whining, pacing, slobbering, howling, and fasting when he finds one.

Altering won't make your dog a wimp, and it won't make your dog fat unless you feed him or her too much. So unless your Golden is an outstanding example of the breed and you're fully committed to his or her puppies, there's just no good reason not to have him or her altered.

Vaccinating Against Disease

A newborn puppy whose mother is healthy and properly vaccinated receives some immunity to disease from the antibodies in *colostrum,* a substance produced by the breasts for a few days after birth. This early protection wears off, however, sometime between the fifth and tenth

FAMILY-FRIENDLY TIP

Kids and the Vet

Taking a beloved pet to the veterinarian can be scary for a child. Fortunately, it can also be an opportunity to teach the child about responsible pet ownership and the importance of regular health care (for people as well as dogs). Before the visit, explain that regular checkups and vaccinations are a good way to prevent sickness, and explain what the vet will be doing as she examines your dog. Encourage your child to pet your dog to help keep both of them more relaxed.

Vet visits also offer an opportunity to teach children how to be safe around pets. Explain that some pets are nervous when they visit the vet, and teach your child never to touch any animal without receiving permission first from the owner.

weeks, leaving the puppies vulnerable at just about the time most of them go to their new homes. This means that vaccinations are vital to your Golden's health.

Puppy vaccinations traditionally are given in a series beginning between 5 and 12 weeks of age, followed by annual boosters. Try not to let your puppy be exposed to diseases carried by other dogs, particularly in public places, until he's fully vaccinated.

The Vaccination Controversy

There is considerable disagreement about the proper approach to lifelong vaccination. Some vets believe that puppy vaccines are effective for the life of the dog, while others recommend booster vaccinations at various intervals. Still others prefer to check a dog's immunity levels by testing the blood for antibodies every year. Of course, some veterinarians and breeders still follow the older vaccination protocols, which call for annual vaccinations. The best thing you can do for your dog's health and your own peace of mind is to learn what you can about vaccination, and speak with your vet about her recommendations for your dog. If you're uncomfortable with one vet's approach, find another vet.

Types of Vaccines

Most canine vaccines are injected subcutaneously (under the skin) or intramuscularly (into the muscle). A few are given in nasal sprays. Dogs are typically vaccinated against some or all of the following diseases.

Canine Distemper

Canine distemper is a highly contagious, highly lethal viral disease of dogs. Distemper causes respiratory problems, vomiting, and diarrhea and may affect the nervous system. The disease is fatal to most puppies and about half of adult dogs who contract it. Dogs who survive are often partly or completely paralyzed and may lose some or all of their vision, hearing, and sense of smell. Puppies are given a

Puppy vaccinations are usually given in a series, followed by annual boosters.

series of three or four vaccinations against distemper.

Canine Bordetellosis (Kennel Cough)

Canine bordetellosis (bordetella, or kennel cough—see also canine parainfluenza) is a bacterial disease of the respiratory tract that causes a horrible cough that is sometimes accompanied by nasal discharge. Kennel cough normally isn't serious in an otherwise healthy adult dog, but it can kill a puppy, elderly dog, or a dog in poor health. The value of vaccination against bordetella for healthy adult dogs is debated by many vets and owners, because the vaccination is not effective against all strains of the disease. When given, the vaccination is usually in the form of a nasal spray.

Canine Leptospirosis

Canine leptospirosis, or "lepto," is a potentially fatal bacterial disease of the kidneys that causes vomiting, vision problems, convulsions, and sometimes kidney failure. It is spread in urine. The disease appears as several different strains but is rare in most areas of the country. Because the risk of exposure is low for most dogs, and serious reactions to the vaccine relatively common, many vets and owners do not vaccinate against lepto. If your dog is at risk of exposure to the disease, consider having the vaccine given separately from the others, and keep your dog at

Pet Insurance

Several companies provide canine health insurance. Coverage and cost vary widely, as does customer satisfaction. Before you buy insurance for your Golden, ask your veterinarian for information, and ask your dog-owning friends for feedback on their satisfaction with coverage from different companies. A better option may be to set up a savings account to be used only for a canine medical emergency. If you need the money, it will be there, and if you don't use it, you don't lose it.

the clinic for half an hour after it's given in case of a negative reaction.

Canine Parainfluenza

Canine parainfluenza (sometimes called kennel cough—see also bordetellosis) is a viral infection of the respiratory tract characterized by coughing. It is spread via nasal and oral secretions of infected dogs. Puppies usually receive a series of three vaccinations, often in combination with other vaccines.

Canine Parvovirus (CPV)

Canine parvovirus (CPV), or "parvo," is a highly contagious viral disease that attacks the intestinal tract, heart muscle, and white blood cells, causing vomiting, severe and foul-smelling

Feeling Good

Golden Retrievers

diarrhea, depression, high fever, and loss of appetite. It is often fatal within a few days of initial symptoms. Puppies who survive parvo can suffer permanent heart damage. The virus is spread through contact with the feces of infected dogs, is easily transported from one place to another on shoes, paws, and clothing, and is very difficult to eradicate. Puppies usually receive a series of three parvo vaccinations.

Infectious Canine Hepatitis

Infectious canine hepatitis is a viral disease that attacks the liver and other tissues. It is spread in the urine and eye secretions of affected dogs. Mild cases are characterized by loss of appetite, depression, mild fever, and frequently a

bluish cast to the cornea of the eye. In severe cases, especially in puppies, symptoms may include abdominal pain, vomiting, diarrhea, edema (swelling) of the head and neck, and sometimes jaundice. Severe cases are often fatal. Puppies usually receive a series of three shots.

Rabies

Rabies is a viral disease that attacks the central nervous system of warm-blooded animals, including people. It is commonly transmitted to domestic animals from wild animals and is always fatal once symptoms appear, which may not occur for several weeks or even months after exposure. Rabies is widespread in North America and some other parts of the world, so laws in most states require that dogs and cats be vaccinated against the disease annually in some states and every three years in others.

Rabies takes two forms. Rabid animals are usually thought of as raging, foaming at the mouth, and aggressive—some of the symptoms of the *furious* form, which occurs late in the progression of the disease. However, animals who have the *dumb* form of rabies may exhibit depression, loss of appetite, subtle behavioral changes, itching, and other symptoms that may indicate any of a number of diseases. Your puppy should have his first rabies vaccination at approximately four months of age and then receive boosters as required.

Parasites

Parasites, disgusting though they may be, are just part of life. Some parasites cause no damage to the host animal and may actually be beneficial. Others cause serious damage and even death. Dogs, like most animals (including people), are potential hosts to a number of external parasites that live on the skin and hair, as well as internal parasites that live in the bloodstream and tissues of the body.

External Parasites

Several species of insects and arthropods make their living by eating the blood and tissue of animals, including dogs. They typically cause severe itching, leading to open sores that are vulnerable to secondary infection, and the parasites themselves often carry diseases from one host animal to another. Not only are they annoying, but they're also dangerous, so it's important to keep your Golden as free of them as possible.

Fleas

Fleas are tiny blood-sucking insects with hard shells that are red, black, or brown. Fleas lay their eggs in grass, carpets, rugs, bedding, and occasionally on the host animal. The eggs usually hatch in 4 to 21 days, but

55

Check your Golden thoroughly for fleas and ticks after he has been playing outside.

How to Remove a Tick

To remove a tick, dab it with alcohol, iodine, or a strong saline solution to make it loosen its grip, and then, with a tick remover, tweezers, or your fingers and a tissue, pull straight out. Don't squeeze—that can force disease-laden fluid into the host. You should see a small bite hole in the skin; a black spot means that you have left the head. Either way, clean the spot with alcohol or antibacterial cleanser, dry, and apply antibacterial ointment. Wash your hands and implement. Check for signs of infection for a few days, particularly if the head was left behind, and see your vet if the area becomes inflamed.

they can survive as long as 18 months before hatching. Flea larvae can also survive long periods, finally emerging as adult fleas when temperature or vibration from a nearby host tells them that food is available. Fleas spread disease and tapeworm larvae, and many dogs are allergic to flea saliva, which will cause them to scratch themselves raw. Fleas will bite people, too.

The most common sign that your dog has fleas is scratching and biting at his skin, which can quickly result in open sores. If you comb your Golden with a flea comb (made with the tines spaced closely together), you may catch some of the little creatures. You may also spot small, black dots on your dog's skin if you separate the hair. You can test the dots by adding a little water; if they turn red or pink, they are "flea dirt"—the blood-laden excrement of fleas.

If you find fleas on your dog or in your house or yard, talk to your vet. Over-the-counter flea controls are not the most effective or cost-efficient treatments, and they can be dangerous. For effective flea control, you need to treat all your pets as well as their environment, and it's important to be sure that all products you use are safe alone and in combination with other products.

Mange

Mange refers to several distinct skin disorders caused by different species of tiny mites that eat skin debris, hair follicles, and tissue. Mange causes hair loss, crusty, irritated skin, and severe itching. Affected dogs often scratch themselves raw, opening the way for viral, fungal, bacterial, or parasitic infections. Some types of mange are contagious; some are not. Home remedies are not very effective, so if you think your dog may have mange, see your vet.

Ticks

Ticks are small blood-sucking arthropods (relatives of spiders and mites). They are usually round and flat, but if they're full of blood or eggs, they look like beans with eight legs. Ticks carry diseases, including Rocky Mountain spotted fever and ehrlichiosis. The deer tick spreads Lyme disease, which can cause debilitating arthritis in a dog (or a person). Deer ticks are tiny and very hard to detect until they are engorged with blood, and by that time they've passed along any disease organisms they carry. Ask your vet about the risk of Lyme disease where you live.

Ticks can be picked up in tall grass, brush, and wooded areas and carried into your own yard and home. If you walk your dog where ticks are likely to be, check him afterward. You may be able to remove the ticks before they bite. If you regularly find ticks, ask your vet about an effective prevention program.

Internal Parasites

Some internal parasites have virtually no effect on the host animal's health, but others cause illness and even death if they are present in large enough numbers. Intestinal parasites can be identified through microscopic examination of the host's feces, and effective treatment prescribed based on the type of parasite—one wormer does not kill all worms. Puppies should have fecal exams when they're vaccinated, and adults should have fecal exams at least once a year. If you see signs of

A puppy can contract hookworms through his mother's milk in the first few weeks of life.

worms in your dog's stools or around his anus, take a specimen to your vet.

Giardia

Giardia are protozoa (single-celled organisms) that infest the intestines and cause diarrhea or bloody or mucus-covered stools accompanied by excess gas, particularly in puppies. Infected dogs pass cysts that contain giardia in their stools, and they can be ingested by other dogs, who then become infected. In a healthy adult dog, the protozoa may cause no problems, but in puppies or dogs with poor nutrition or other health issues, they can be a serious health hazard. Veterinary diagnosis and treatment are essential to rid your dog of giardia.

Hookworms

Hookworms are tiny worms that can, in large numbers, suck enough blood from the walls of the intestine to cause anemia, especially in puppies. A dog can acquire hookworms in several ways. One way is through ingestion. Another way is if the larvae burrow through his skin or enter through the placenta prior to birth. He can also get hookworms through his mother's milk in the first few weeks of life.

Hookworms are diagnosed through

Adequate exercise is vital for your Golden's physical and mental health.

microscopic examination of feces, and they are relatively easy to treat. Hookworm larvae can burrow into human skin, too, which causes itching, but the larvae rarely mature in people.

Heartworms

Heartworm disease is caused by a parasitic worm that infests the host animal's heart, clogging the vessels and causing congestive heart failure. In the early stages of heartworm infection, a dog will show no symptoms. Eventually, a cough will develop, and as the infection worsens, the dog will become exercise-intolerant, and the lungs will sound abnormal through a stethoscope. Symptoms of severe heartworm infection include these symptoms in addition to difficulty breathing, enlargement of the liver, temporary loss of consciousness from poor blood flow to the brain, fluid accumulation in the abdomen, abnormal heart sounds, and eventually, death. Treatment for the disease is aimed at killing the worms in the heart, which can be hard on the dog.

Mosquitoes carry heartworm larvae from infected dogs to new victims. Ask your vet about the risk of heartworm disease where you live and travel with your dog. If your dog is at risk, your vet will prescribe a heartworm preventive and will suggest that your dog be tested for heartworms every year or two.

Ringworm

Ringworm is a fungus that causes bald patches that often look raw. Like many fungal infections, ringworm is difficult to cure. It's also highly contagious and can spread to people. If your Golden develops any sort of bald spot, take him to the vet. Don't wait to see if it gets better or waste time with home remedies— you may end up with a much bigger problem.

Roundworms

Roundworms, which look like strings of spaghetti up to 8 inches (20 cm) in length, are common. Even puppies from responsible breeders with clean facilities and healthy dogs often have roundworms, because if the mother has had roundworms at any time in her life, she can pass them to her puppies before or after they're born. Testing the mother for roundworms before breeding or whelping won't reveal roundworm larvae that are encysted in her muscle tissue or mammary glands, and nursing puppies can ingest roundworm larvae in their mother's milk. Puppies may also pick up the parasites by ingesting roundworm eggs, which can be passed on by a wide variety of other animals, including earthworms, cockroaches, rodents, poultry, and other dogs.

A large or chronic infection of roundworms will cause a puppy to develop a potbelly, have diarrhea, and vomit. At first, he'll seem to be hungry all the time, because the roundworms eat the food digesting in the pup's intestines. Eventually, the puppy will become so malnourished and weak that he will stop eating. Fortunately, roundworms are easy to eliminate with the proper medication. Humans can get roundworms, too, so practice careful hygiene until your vet declares your puppy free of worms, and teach your children to do the same.

Tapeworms

Tapeworms require two different hosts during their life cycle. Tapeworm larvae inhabit intermediate hosts such as a mice, rabbits, and fleas. If your dog ingests such an infected animal or insect, the larvae then develop into adult tapeworms in your dog's intestines, where they eat digesting food and grow to several feet (m) in length. Tapeworms usually do not show up in fecal specimens and are diagnosed instead when ricelike segments break off of the worm and stick to the tissue and hair around the dog's anus. If you see signs of tapeworm on your dog, talk to your vet—a special wormer is required to kill tapeworm. If your Golden kills and eats wild animals or has had a case of fleas, be especially alert for tapeworm evidence.

Whipworms

Whipworms look like bits of thread, long and thin. They are hard to diagnose because they are rarely seen in the feces, and they shed few eggs. Diagnosis is usually based on chronic weight loss and feces with a mucus-like covering. Whipworms are hard to eradicate, and several treatments by your vet may be necessary.

Health Issues in Golden Retrievers

It is to your advantage to be aware of hereditary problems to which

Most Goldens are healthy, and regular veterinary care will help keep them that way.

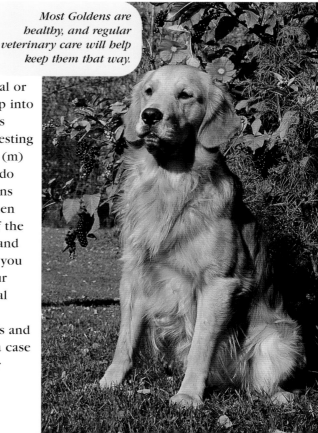

Golden Retrievers

Goldens are susceptible, so that you'll know what to look for if your dog becomes ill. The conditions described here are those noted by the Golden Retriever Club of America (GRCA) as the more common problems in the breed. Don't panic, though— most Goldens are healthy! To keep it that way, all Golden Retrievers used for breeding should be screened for inherited diseases, and affected dogs should not be bred.

If you suspect that your Golden has an ear infection, see your vet.

Cancer

Cancers are among the most commonly reported life-threatening health problems in Golden Retrievers. Although most cancers strike when a dog is between 8 and 13 years of age, some occur in much younger dogs. The prognosis for a Golden diagnosed with cancer depends in part on the type of cancer, the age and previous health status of the dog, and how early the disease is detected. Some cancers, like squamous cell carcinoma, have a fairly high cure rate, while others, like osteosarcoma, are harder to cure. Treatment options for dogs are essentially the same as for people: surgery, chemotherapy, and radiation therapy.

Some cancers are completely preventable. Females who are spayed have no risk for ovarian or uterine cancer, and males who are castrated have no risk for testicular cancer. In addition, according to the health survey of the GRCA, spaying a female before her first heat reduces the risk of breast cancer by about 95 percent.

Ear Problems

Goldens are prone to infections of the ears because their beautiful soft ear "leathers" (the floppy part) hold moisture in the ear canal, creating an ideal environment for bacteria and yeast to grow. Allergies can also lead to ear infections. Periodic ear cleaning will help minimize your dog's risk of ear problems (see Chapter 4) and is especially important if your dog swims or plays in water. If you suspect that your Golden has an ear infection, see your vet; effective treatment depends on proper diagnosis.

How Canine Hips Are Evaluated

Two programs are recognized in the United States for evaluating canine hip structure. The Orthopedic Foundation for Animals (OFA) rates the structure of hips by evaluating X rays. To be certified, the dog must be at least 24 months old when x-rayed. The OFA ratings of Excellent, Good, and Fair mean that the dog is free of hip dysplasia.

The Pennsylvania Hip Improvement Program (PennHIP) evaluates puppies as young as four months old using a "distraction index" for each hip, indicating the laxity, or looseness, of the hip joint, which is considered an accurate predictor of degenerative joint disease. PennHIP also ranks each dog's hips in relation to all members of his breed who have been evaluated by PennHIP.

symptoms of hypothyroidism can indicate other problems. The only way to be certain is through laboratory tests. A simple thyroid test (T4) is often performed, but the results are not very reliable. A complete panel measuring Total T4, free T4 (the usable T4 in the blood), TGAA (thyroglobulin autoantibodies), cTSH (canine thyroid stimulating hormone), and sometimes T3 and free T3 is more accurate. Thyroid disease is slow to develop, and a dog who tests negative now may test positive in a year or two. Treatment with a hormone supplement, most often L-thyroxine, is relatively inexpensive and usually effective.

Endocrine System Problems

One endocrine system disorder that can affect Goldens is called hypothyroidism, which is characterized by a lack of sufficient thyroid hormone. This disease can negatively affect a dog's physical and emotional life. Symptoms include hair loss, obesity or weight gain, lethargy, inflamed ears, abnormally cool skin, and itchy, inflamed, crusty, or scaly skin. Hypothyroidism can be hard to diagnose, because other conditions can affect hormone levels, and many

Eye Problems

All Goldens used for breeding should be examined annually by a board-certified veterinary ophthalmologist to rule out hereditary eye disease.

Cataracts

One of the most common hereditary eye diseases is hereditary cataracts, opaque growths that cover the lens of the eye, causing partial or complete blindness. (Not all cataracts are inherited—they can also be caused by injury, illness, and aging.) Cataracts can be removed surgically.

Central Progressive Retinal Atrophy (CPRA)

Central Progressive Retinal Atrophy (CPRA) causes the retina (the light-receptive part of the eye) to deteriorate, resulting in partial or complete blindness. There is no treatment at present.

Retinal Dysplasia

Retinal dysplasia causes the retina to detach, again causing loss of vision. There is no effective treatment at present.

Other Eye Disorders

Other problems affect the eyelashes and eyelids, including entropion (the eyelid turns in toward the eye), ectropion (the eyelid turns out), and trichiasis and distichiasis (eyelashes or hairs rub against the eye, causing irritation, abrasion, and potentially, infection). These conditions may require surgery to prevent permanent damage to the eye.

Heart Disease

Subvalvular aortic stenosis (SAS) occurs in some families of Goldens. The left ventricle of the heart pumps oxygenated blood through the aortic valve and into the aorta, from which it then flows throughout the body before returning to the lungs for reoxygenation. *Stenosis* refers to a narrowing of the aortic valve, which reduces blood flow, causing the dog to faint or even die. A heart murmur may indicate SAS, so examination by a

Keep your Golden at a healthy weight, and he'll live a longer, happier life.

veterinary cardiologist is recommended if a murmur is detected. A Golden should also be examined before breeding.

Neurological Problems

Epilepsy is a disorder that affects some Goldens. It is characterized by seizures, or "fits," although seizures can also be caused by toxic chemicals, drugs, heatstroke, head injuries, or disease. When no clear cause can be established for seizures, they are usually attributed to primary or idiopathic epilepsy, which is considered to be genetic. Seizures are rarely fatal, although frequent, uncontrollable seizures can lead to hyperthermia, hypoglycemia, exhaustion, brain damage, and even death. Epilepsy cannot be cured, but most cases can be controlled with medication.

Orthopedic Problems

Research has shown a significant relationship between excess weight, especially in puppies, and the occurrence of musculoskeletal conditions, including hip and elbow dysplasia. So don't let your Golden get fat at any age—he'll live a longer, healthier life.

The following are some common orthopedic problems found in the Golden Retriever.

Canine Hip Dysplasia (CHD)

Canine hip dysplasia, or CHD, is a potentially crippling inherited condition in which the bones of the hip joint do not fit together properly, making the dog susceptible to painful arthritis. You cannot tell if a dog has CHD by watching him move. In fact, some affected dogs show no symptoms of dysplasia until they are several years old, which is why dogs used for breeding should first be x-rayed to be sure their hip joints are properly formed. Treatment for CHD depends on the severity of the symptoms, and surgery is often recommended. In mild cases, weight control, moderate exercise, dietary supplements, and pain relievers as needed may be enough to keep symptoms under control.

Elbow Dysplasia (ED)

Elbow dysplasia (ED) refers to any of several inherited malformations of the bones of the elbow joint. ED is thought to affect about ten percent of Golden Retrievers. Symptoms can appear at any age and include lameness, limited range of motion, and a pigeon-toed look as the dog turns his toes inward to compensate for elbow pain. Treatment is similar to that for hip dysplasia.

Skin Problems

The hardest part of dealing with allergies and hot spots is identifying the cause. Keep an open mind, and if possible, eliminate the source of your dog's problem rather than simply treating the symptoms with drugs.

Hot spots—inflamed areas of skin that often become open sores—are common in Goldens and can have a variety of causes, including chemicals found in lawn and garden products, flea or tick medications, shampoos and other coat products, and some housecleaning products. Allergic reactions to flea saliva are also a common cause, which is another reason that flea control is essential. In addition, food allergies affect many Goldens. (See Chapter 3.)

Hot spots are common in Goldens and can be caused by a variety of factors, including shampoos and other coat products.

Hot spots can be difficult to clear up, so see your vet for help as soon as you notice the problem. This is so that you can rule out causes such as mange or ringworm and begin effective treatment, which often involves a change in food, topical ointments or drying agents, and possibly injections.

First Aid

Complete information on how to respond to an emergency is beyond the scope of this book, so consider adding a good veterinary first-aid book to your home library, or take a pet first-aid or cardiopulmonary resuscitation (CPR) course. You can prevent many emergencies by following simple rules of responsible pet care, including the following:

- Keep your Golden on leash when not fenced or indoors.
- Keep toxic substances out of reach.
- In hot weather, never leave your dog in a vehicle or restrict his exercise. Be sure that he has shade and fresh water.

Common Canine Emergencies

In any emergency, provide first aid, and then get your Golden to a veterinarian as quickly as possible. Call ahead so the office knows you're on your way, and drive carefully.

Fractures are not uncommon in active dogs.

Here are some common canine emergencies:

Cuts, Bites, and Bleeding

Cuts, bites, and bleeding are common in active dogs. Clean minor injuries gently with clear water, and apply pressure with a clean towel or gauze pad until the bleeding slows or stops. Apply a topical antibiotic ointment, and watch the wound for a few days for signs of infection. If it is bleeding and is deep or long, apply pressure and get your dog to your vet. If your dog gets bitten by another animal, clean the wound, stop the bleeding if necessary, and call your vet. Bite wounds introduce bacteria from the mouth and may also introduce disease, including rabies. Even if the wound doesn't require veterinary care, your vet will probably prescribe an oral antibiotic.

Fractures

Fractures (broken bones) are also not uncommon in active dogs. If you think your Golden has a fracture, keep him quiet, carry him (preferably on a blanket or board) to a vehicle, and get him to a veterinarian. Don't try to apply a splint—you could cause more damage. Veterinary care is essential for all fractures.

Heatstroke

Heatstroke (hyperthermia) occurs when an animal's body temperature rises beyond a safe range. Symptoms include red or pale gums, a bright red tongue, sticky and thick saliva, rapid panting, vomiting, and diarrhea. The dog may act dizzy or weak, and he may go into shock. Heatstroke can kill your dog or cause serious, permanent injury. If you suspect heatstroke, wrap your dog in a cool, wet towel or blanket, and get him to a vet.

Poisons

Poisons are all around your Golden and are present in medications, chocolate, raisins and grapes, hundreds of plants, fertilizers, herbicides, insecticides, slug bait, rodenticides, lead (found in paint chips or dust, toys, drapery weights, fishing weights, lead shot, some tiles, some types of insulation, improperly glazed ceramic bowls, water passed through lead pipes, and more), antifreeze, spiders, snakes, and many other things. Symptoms of poisoning may include vomiting, diarrhea, loss of appetite, swelling of the tongue and other mouth tissues or of the face or body, excessive salivation, and staggering, seizures, or collapse. If you think that your dog has been poisoned, contact your veterinarian, emergency clinic, or animal poison center immediately. Delaying treatment could make the difference between life and death.

Alternative Therapies

The terms *alternative, complementary,* or *holistic* medicine

SENIOR DOG TIP

Living With a Senior

Every individual ages differently, but you'll probably start to see age-related changes when your Golden is around seven or eight years old. He may slow down a bit and become stiff in his movements and less tolerant of changes in his environment and routine. He may lose some or all of his hearing and vision, and his body may take on a bony feel as he loses weight and muscle mass. Some older dogs suffer from separation anxiety, and most sleep longer and more deeply than when they were young.

Regular, gentle grooming will help keep your old dog's coat and skin in good condition, stimulate circulation, and alert you to lumps and bumps that need veterinary attention. Regular walks are good for his physical and mental health, as long as your Golden is up to them. Regular checkups are also essential for older dogs, and a sudden or extreme change in your Golden's physical condition or behavior also warrants a trip to the vet. Your Golden will hopefully be part of your life for more than a decade if you give him good care and lots of love.

Feeling Good

cover a wide range of practices loosely connected by a common belief that emotional and physical factors work together to promote health or illness. Among the alternative approaches to veterinary care are the formal disciplines of chiropractic, acupuncture, homeopathy, herbal therapy, and nutrition, as well as such practices as massage therapy, shiatsu, reiki, TTouch, contact reflex, and others. If you're interested in alternative veterinary care for your dog, be cautious. Some practices and practitioners are safe and useful, but some can be ineffective or dangerous.

Acupuncture

Acupuncture is an ancient Chinese form of treatment in which fine sterile needles are inserted into key points in the body to stimulate health and healing. Acupuncture may be used to treat injuries and illnesses. For more information and to find a veterinary acupuncturist, visit the website for the American Academy of Veterinary Acupuncture at www.aava.org.

Herbal Therapy

Herbal therapy involves the use of plant materials to treat illness or injury and to support good health. If you plan to give your dog herbs, be cautious and consult your veterinarian. Some herbs will do no harm, and some may help. But some herbs can cause serious problems or even kill your dog—even herbs that are safe for human use may harm your

If you suspect that your dog may have been poisoned, get help immediately.

dog. Keep in mind, too, that herbs are not regulated by the Food and Drug Administration (FDA), and claims made by manufacturers may or may not be accurate. For more information and to find a veterinarian trained in the use of herbs, visit the website of the Veterinary Botanical Medical Association at www.vbma.org.

Homeopathy

Homeopathic medicine is based on the principle that like affects like. In other words, very small amounts of substances are given to stimulate the animal's immune system so that healing can take place. Homeopathy is often used along with other forms of holistic care. For more information, visit the website of the American Holistic Veterinary Medical Association at www.ahvma.org.

Good health care is worth its weight in Goldens and will keep your dog healthier throughout his life. Work in partnership with your vet, and your Golden Retriever should be a part of your own life for a decade or longer.

First-Aid Kit for Dogs

The following are some items that you should have on hand in case an emergency arises:
• A muzzle to keep your dog from biting when frightened or in pain;
• Antidiarrheal (ask your vet's advice);
• Artificial tear gel to lubricate eyes after flushing;
• Bulb syringe or medicine syringe;
• Forceps or tweezers;
• Good basic veterinary first-aid manual;
• Hydrogen peroxide in 3% solution (USP). Write the purchase date on the bottle, and replace with a fresh bottle once a year;
• Mild grease-cutting dishwashing liquid to remove skin contaminants;
• Rubber gloves for handling a contaminated dog;
• Saline eye solution to flush eyes;
• Small notebook and pen or pencil for taking notes (for instance, time poison was ingested, time of a seizure, intervals between seizures, bowel movements, vomiting, etc.);
• Telephone numbers for your veterinarian, closest emergency veterinary facility, National Animal Poison Control Center (NAPCC)—1-888-4ANI-HELP or 1-900-443-0000—and a friend or neighbor who could help in an emergency;
• Topical antibiotic.

Being Good

Nearly everything your Golden Retriever does is learned or instinctive. (A few behaviors may be caused by illness, injury, or chemicals.) You can't do anything about his instincts, but you can—and should—guide your Golden's behavior with training.

What Is Dog Training, Anyway?

Training is the process of teaching your dog new habits. Your Golden is always learning, whether you think you're training him or not, and if he does something successfully more than two or three times, it's likely to become a habit. It is easier to promote good habits than to change bad ones once they're established, and it's easier to teach your dog to do something acceptable than to do nothing at all. If you also teach him that learning is fun and that you're a fair and trustworthy guide, your Golden will learn quickly and live to please you.

The most effective and fair way to train your dog is to reward him for doing what you want him to do—this is called *positive reinforcement*. Encourage everyone in your household to follow the same rules, and use the same words and methods for training your Golden so that he won't be confused.

Training Tools

The following are some of the most common items you will need to train your Golden.

Training Collar

First, your dog needs a training collar, which won't be the collar he wears all the time with his tags. The type of collar you use will depend on your dog's age, personality, and level of training; your training skills; and the type of training you're doing. Here are some common training collars:

Choke Chain

Choke chains (slip or training collars) are made of metal links, nylon, or leather. Used incorrectly, choke chains can damage your dog's neck and throat. An experienced dog trainer can use a choke chain without hurting a dog, but these collars are often misused, making the choke chain

Use positive reinforcement to reward your dog for a job well done.

dangerous and ineffective for training and control.

Flat Collar

A *flat collar* is made of leather, nylon, or fabric and closes with a buckle or quick-release fastener. This is the only type of collar that should be used on a young puppy and is the one your dog should wear with his tags.

Halter (Head Collar)

A *halter* (or *head collar*) controls a dog by controlling his head. Halters give so much control that people often use them without training their dogs and then have no control without the halters.

Leash

You also need at least one leash. Most experienced trainers prefer leather leashes because they're strong, flexible, and easy on the hands. For training your Golden, you will probably want a 4- to 6-foot (1.2 to 1.8 m) leash that's ½ to 1 inch (1.3 to 2.54 cm) wide.

Treats and Toys

Finally, you need some treats and toys that your dog really likes so that you can reward him for learning.

Socialization and Growing Up

Socialization is an essential part of your Golden's education. He needs to meet all kinds of people—old, young, male, female, different races, bearded, and

Training Treats

Treats used in training should be something your dog likes: cooked meat, tiny bits of raw carrot and green bean, cheese, cereal, fruit (no grapes or raisins—they're toxic to dogs), and of course, commercial or homemade dog treats. Keep the pieces tiny and fairly soft so that your dog can scarf down a treat and keep training without having to stop and chew. Don't give treats away free—have your dog do something to earn each one.

clean shaven—as well as nonaggressive dogs and other animals, and to experience as many sights and sounds as possible, so that he will be more confident and comfortable throughout his life. Socialization is particularly important when your dog is between 7 and 14 weeks old, but the process should continue throughout puberty and young adulthood.

During adolescence, your dog may forget his manners. Think of him as the canine version of a teenager and his behavior will make more sense. Be sure he gets plenty of physical exercise, repeat earlier obedience lessons, and be patient, firm, and consistent, and you'll come out the other end of this period with a lovely adult Golden.

Crate Training

Proper use of a crate will keep your dog and your belongings safe until he's trustworthy in your absence. Most dogs quickly accept their crates, and many lie in them by choice. Dogs are by nature den animals, and a cozy crate is a safe, comfortable, quiet "den."

Choose a crate that's large enough for your Golden to stand, turn around, and lie down. For most adult Goldens, 24 by 36 inches (61.0 by 91.4 cm) is adequate, although if your grown dog will be confined for longer than an hour at a time, you may want to give him a larger crate. However, if you're housetraining a puppy, use a smaller crate or partition an adult-size crate to limit the usable space. A healthy dog won't relieve himself where he sleeps, and a smaller space makes it harder to relieve himself at one end of the crate and lie down at the other. If your pup likes to rip things up, don't give him any bedding, and don't use newspaper or weewee pads in the crate.

How to Crate Train Your Golden

To teach your Golden to go willingly into his crate, toss a toy or treat in and say, "Crate" or "Kennel." Give him a chew toy and possibly a hollow bone

Socialization is a crucial part of your Golden puppy's learning experience.

stuffed with something good like cheese and kibble. Feed him his meals in his crate, at least for a while, and if possible, put his crate in your bedroom at night so that he won't feel isolated. Remember, he's a pack animal and you're his pack.

If your pup or new adult dog whines or barks when he's locked in his crate, hold out until he's quiet, and then reward him with praise and a treat while he's still in the crate. Don't let him out when he makes a fuss (unless you think he needs to relieve himself)—he'll learn that noise opens the door. Wait until he's quiet to let him out.

Your dog should think of his crate as a good, safe place, so don't use it for punishment.

Housetraining

If you're careful to take your puppy out when he needs to relieve himself and patient when he has the occasional accident, housetraining should progress

quickly. Remember that your puppy doesn't have complete control of his bladder or bowels, and by the time he knows he has to go, he may not be able to hold it any longer. It's your job—not his—to teach him where he should relieve himself and to prevent accidents.

Puppies less than six months old urinate every two to four hours and defecate several times a day, including during the night, so crating your pup where you can hear him when you're sleeping is important. Typically, a puppy needs to go after or during every meal, first thing in the morning, last thing at night, after sleeping, and after active play. To estimate your puppy's endurance, take his age in months, add one, and translate into hours. Thus, if your pup is two months old, he can probably go three hours between potty breaks. A healthy older dog can usually last seven or eight hours.

How to Housetrain Your Golden

To teach your Golden where to go, take him on lead to the place you want him to use, and wait. If he doesn't go within 5 minutes, crate him for 10 to 15 minutes, and then take him out again.

The Expert Knows

How to Talk "Dog"

Your tone of voice and body language communicate more than words to your Golden Retriever. Dogs like happy voices, so keep your tone cheerful. Dogs also pay close attention to posture and movement, so stand upright, relax, and be confident when you train. Your dog will feel better, and you will, too!

housetrained, the training procedures are the same, with the added benefit that your dog should have better control for longer periods of time, and he can keep control long enough to walk out the door.

Housetraining Accidents

Chances are your dog will have at least one accident while he's learning. *Never* yell or punish him, and *never ever* rub his nose in it. Such methods are abusive, and they don't work. Take him out in case he hasn't finished, and then clean up and remind yourself to supervise your dog more closely. If he smells urine or feces, he'll think he's found the toilet,

When he relieves himself, praise him and give him a treat or short playtime. Puppies don't always finish the job right away, so give him a little time. When he's loose in the house, confine him to the room you're in, and *watch him closely*. Turning in circles, sniffing the floor, or arching his back while walking are all potty signals, so pick him up immediately and take him out.

If you've adopted an adult Golden who isn't

To teach your Golden where to eliminate, first take him on lead to the place that you want him to use.

so it's vital that you remove all trace of odor. Regular cleaners won't fool your Golden's marvelous nose, but you can purchase special products from pet supply stores to neutralize the odor.

Be patient. It can take several months to train a puppy or untrained adult to be fully reliable. Regardless of his age, if your dog doesn't seem to have normal control of his bladder and bowels, talk to your vet—urinary tract infections, parasites, and other problems can cause control problems.

If you have to be gone longer than your dog's capacity to "hold it," consider hiring a reliable pet sitter or dog walker to exercise him during the day. It's not fair or realistic to ask a dog of any age to wait beyond his capacity or to lie in his own waste.

Housetraining Tips

Your dog will housetrain more easily if you adhere to the following:

- Feed him a high-quality dry food to promote better bowel control and smaller, more compact stools.
- Don't give him the run of the house until he's reliable. Keep him with you and watch him closely. When you can't watch him, put him into his crate.
- Feed and exercise him on a regular schedule.
- Feed him at least four hours before bedtime, and don't let him drink water within two hours of bedtime.

Finding a Good Obedience Instructor

You can learn a lot about dog training from books, magazines, and the Internet, but nothing can replace a good obedience class taught by a qualified instructor. To find a class, ask your veterinarian, breeder, and dog-owning friends for recommendations, or do an Internet search for "dog obedience" and your city. If possible, observe a class or two before you sign up, and if you don't like what you see, look elsewhere.

- Keep his potty area free of feces. He doesn't want to step in it any more than you do.

Basic Obedience Commands

You can teach your Golden many things, but there are a few basics that will make him a nice dog to live with.

Sit

A dog who will sit (and stay sitting) on command is a dog you can control, whether you are waiting for a green light when out for a walk or trying to put a food bowl on the floor without being mobbed by a hungry Golden. The *sit* command provides a quick alternative behavior for a dog who is about to do something you don't want, like planting muddy feet on your clean pants!

How to Teach Sit

Start with your dog on leash. Hold a small treat in front of his nose, *slowly* raise it just enough to clear his head, and move it slowly toward his tail. As his head comes up, his fanny has to go down (unless you lift the treat too high—then he'll probably jump for it). Say "sit" as you move the treat slowly backward. The instant your Golden's behind hits the floor, praise him and give him the treat. If he stands up before you give him the treat, don't give it to him. Have him sit again, and give him the treat while he's sitting. Repeat three or four times, and then quit. Do several repetitions during the day.

When your dog sits promptly on command, slowly increase the length of time he has to sit to get the treat. Eventually, you can wean away the treat most of the time and reward him just with praise, but give him a goody once in a while to keep the game interesting for him.

Come

You no doubt want your dog to come when you call him. Who wants to chase a disobedient dog around the backyard in the rain? More important, though, a dog who comes reliably when called is safer than one who doesn't.

The sit *command provides a quick alternative behavior for a dog who is about to do something you don't want.*

How to Teach Come

Start with your Golden on leash. Say "Rover, come!" *only one time* in a happy, playful voice. Do whatever you have to do to get your dog to come to you *without repeating the command*—walk or run the other way, crouch down, and play with a toy. If he still doesn't come, gently pull him in with the leash. If he starts to come on his own, stop pulling. Praise and reward him when he gets to you, and then let him go so that he doesn't learn that coming when called always means the end of the fun. Repeat this command two or three times, and then quit. Do this several times a day.

It all sounds simple, doesn't it? But how many dogs do you know who come reliably when called? Unfortunately, many people accidentally teach their dogs to ignore them instead of teaching them to come when called. Here are some guidelines to help you avoid that:

- Never call your dog for something he finds disagreeable, and *never* punish him after calling him to you. He should believe that with you is the safest, most fun place he can be.

- Always praise your dog for coming when you call, and from time to time give him something he likes: a treat, toy, or belly rub.

- Always use the same word to call your dog; "come" or "here" are

FAMILY-FRIENDLY TIP

Kids and Dog Training

Involving children with your dog's training will help ensure that he understands that the kids outrank him in the pack, and it will help your children understand your dog better. But be realistic. Young Goldens are a handful even for adults, and most children just don't have the strength or skills to manage such a big dog. Although a child can help, an adult must be responsible for your Golden's training. If your child is old enough to sit quietly and obey the rules of a training facility, bring her along to watch your obedience classes. Let her help you with "doggy homework," but be sure a responsible adult is present whenever she works with the dog.

common. Don't confuse him with a string of gibberish.

- Give the *come* command only once. If you repeat it, your dog will learn to ignore you. If he doesn't come, go get him, put his leash on, and go back to leash training. If you don't give him a chance to be wrong, he'll learn to be right.

- Never let your Golden off leash in an unfenced area if he doesn't come *every single time* you call him. Even if you think your dog is reliable, remember that a single lapse in obedience can get him killed.

Stay

Stay tells your dog not to move from a place and position, like *sit, stand,* or *down*, until you say it's okay. Remember to release your dog when it's okay for him to move; use a word such as "free" or "okay" to tell him he's off the hook.

How to Teach Stay

Put your dog in position and tell him "stay." If he moves, put him back in the place and position where he was. Don't repeat the command—he needs to remember what you told him to do. When he has stayed in position a few seconds, praise him, give him a treat, and then release him. Stay close to your dog, and start with short *stays* of less than a minute. Slowly increase the time until he will stay five minutes with you standing close to him. Then move a step or two farther away, have him stay for one minute, and build up again to five minutes. When he does that, add another step or two, shorten the time, and build up again.

The biggest mistake people make in teaching *stay* is trying to increase time and/or distance too quickly. Add one step at a time, and every time you add distance, shorten the time and build back up slowly. If your dog pops

The down *command will help your Golden develop self-control.*

up, fidgets, or whines before the time is up, stand a little closer until he's comfortable again with that distance for that length of time. Remember, your Golden wants to be with you, and it's hard for him to learn to stay away.

Practice in different environments so that your dog learns to stay where you tell him, no matter where you are. Make sure you're always in control; if you're in an unfenced area, keep your dog on a leash.

Down

Teaching your dog to lie down (and stay) when you tell him to gives you even more control than the *sit* command. *Down* is particularly useful when you need your dog to stay out of the way for a while. This command will also help your Golden develop a bit of self-control.

How to Teach Down

You can teach your dog to lie down from a *stand* or a *sit*. Hold a treat in front of your dog's nose, and slowly lower your hand toward the ground while telling him, "Down." As his head follows the treat, he should lie down. If he doesn't, guide him by pushing gently down between his shoulder blades. As soon as he's down, praise him and give him the treat. When he's doing that quickly and reliably, give him the command but don't move your hand toward him. Slowly increase

SENIOR DOG TIP

Can You Train an Older Dog?

It's never too late to begin or renew obedience training. Adult dogs are able to focus longer than puppies, and they usually enjoy the attention they get in training sessions. Some adults who have had no previous training have a little trouble understanding what's expected, but once they "learn to learn," they become eager students.

the length of time that he has to stay down before he gets the treat, and praise and reward him while he's down, not after he jumps up.

Walk Nicely on Leash

You should be able to walk your Golden Retriever on a leash without having him pull your arm off or tie you up. Begin by making sure that your dog's collar fits him properly and that your leash is long enough to give him reasonable freedom of movement but short enough for you to manage comfortably.

If you're having trouble training your Golden, consider an obedience class.

How to Teach Walk Nicely on Leash

If you're training a puppy, or if your Golden is fairly responsive to you, try the "no forward progress" approach first: If your dog pulls, stop and stand still until he stops pulling. It may take him a moment to notice that you're not moving, but when he stops and looks at you, praise him and start walking. If he pulls again, stop. Your walks may be stop-and-go at first, but your dog will soon figure out that pulling makes you stop and walking nicely keeps you moving.

If stopping in place doesn't work, change directions so that your dog learns that he can't predict where you'll go and he needs to pay attention to you. Grasp your leash and set your hands together in front of your waist. When your dog pulls, turn and walk quickly in a different direction. Don't wait for him, and don't talk to him until he catches up. Then praise him, and turn back in the original direction. Most dogs quickly learn to pay attention and stop pulling.

If your Golden is not responsive to these methods, take him to an obedience class (or another one if you've been through one already), so that a knowledgeable instructor can help you find the best equipment and method for gaining better control of your individual dog.

Leave It!

Leave it is a useful command that means "don't touch." To teach this successfully, your dog must learn that it's more rewarding to obey you than not to, and that he'll never get the object he desires anyway. To teach him these things, you need to reward your dog for obeying you, and while you're training him, you must control the situation so he can't get whatever he's after.

Two cautions. First, if your dog tends to guard food or other resources, get help from an experienced dog trainer or a qualified behaviorist. Second, no matter how good your Golden is with kids, teach children never to take things from a dog, even a dog they know. If the dog has something he shouldn't have, the kids should tell an adult.

How to Teach Leave It
To teach *leave it,* put your dog on leash.

Put something that you know your dog will find interesting on or near the floor. (Don't use his regular toys or food—that wouldn't be fair.) Have some special yummy treats ready, like teensy bits of cheese or meat. Walk your dog near the item you've placed on the floor. When he shows interest in it, say, "Leave it," and walk quickly away—he'll have to follow you because of the leash. As soon as your dog looks at you, give him the treat and praise him. Repeat three or four times, and then quit. Don't let your dog get the object, even after your session is finished. Once your Golden learns to leave things alone when you tell him, you won't need to give him treats all the time, but remember to praise him—it isn't easy to resist temptation.

Training your Golden Retriever will take some time and effort, but having a well-trained companion is worth every minute and every biscuit you give. Besides, didn't you get a dog so that you could spend time with him? Training, done with kindness, gentleness, and a positive, motivational attitude, will strengthen the bond between the two of you—and that's what having a dog is all about.

Leave it *is a useful command that means "don't touch."*

83

Chapter 7

In the

Doghouse

Goldens are great dogs who want to please you, but even the most angelic canine's halo slips a little at times. Fortunately, with training, planning, and quick, appropriate responses, you can prevent or eliminate most problem behaviors.

Before we get to specific issues, here are some general questions to ask yourself when behavior issues arise:

- Why is my dog doing what he's doing? Is he acting on an instinct? Is he bored and full of energy? Has he learned that an obnoxious behavior gets him what he wants?
- Am I giving my dog clear direction, or am I confusing him and reinforcing behaviors I don't really want? (Basic training often affects a dog's overall behavior, so consider taking or retaking an obedience class.)
- Am I giving him an acceptable alternative to the behavior I don't want?
- Am I proactive, taking steps to prevent unwanted behaviors before they happen?

Keep in mind that your Golden Retriever does not do naughty things to bug you or get back at you—those are human, not canine, motives. Most behavior issues occur because the dog doesn't understand the human rules. It's your job to teach your dog. If you're as patient and forgiving as a Golden Retriever, you and your dog can overcome most problems and become even better friends in the process.

Now let's look at some of the more common behavior problems and what you can do about them.

Barking

Barking is a natural means of communication for a dog. Your Golden can bark a greeting, a warning, or an invitation to play. Chances are you understand your dog most of the time, and you respond.

Barking is fine as long as it's not excessive, but it can get out of control. Problem barking can be hard to stop, because it's self-rewarding for your dog, but it can usually be curtailed if you're willing to invest some time and effort.

Barking is a natural means of communication for your Golden Retriever.

If Your Golden Gets Lost

If your Golden gets lost, you can improve the odds that he'll come home safe and sound by following a few simple steps.

1. ID your dog. Attach a current name tag, registration tag, and rabies tag to your dog's collar. Since collars and tags can be lost or removed, consider a microchip or tattoo for permanent identification as well. Permanent ID also gives you proof of ownership.
2. Act fast. The sooner you begin a search, the better the chances that you'll find your dog.
3. Call all shelters and veterinarians in your own and nearby areas, and contact your closest Golden Retriever rescue organization. Visit area shelters as often as possible; shelter staff could overlook your dog, so it's important to check in yourself.
4. Advertise in your local newspaper, and consider advertising in newspapers from neighboring towns as well; a lost or stolen dog can turn up a long way from home.
5. Use the Internet to post information about your dog to discussion lists and bulletin boards, and ask readers to forward the information to other appropriate lists.
6. Post flyers with a color photo of your dog, where and when he was lost, and your telephone number around your neighborhood, on store bulletin boards, and wherever else you can stick a poster. Consider carrying copies to neighbors and local businesses, too.
7. Ask neighbors, especially children, to keep an eye out for your dog, and give them your phone number. Kids are more likely than adults to notice a loose dog. Ask area schools for permission to hang your poster where students will see it.

Solution

If your Golden barks too much, first try to find the reason. Is he bored or lonely? Is he excited by things he sees and hears around your home? Finding the reason behind excessive barking may give you a fairly simple solution.

Dogs often bark to sound an alert when they perceive an "intruder." If the person is a burglar, barking is good. If it's your neighbor puttering around his own yard, barking is not so good. Since Goldens are generally friendly, simply introducing your dog to your neighbors may help curb the barking. Teach him that having people around is a good thing. Rather

The Expert Knows

How to Find a Canine Behaviorist

If your Golden Retriever has behavior problems that you can't manage through regular obedience training, a qualified canine behaviorist may be able to help. Unfortunately, anyone can hang out a shingle as a dog trainer or behaviorist, so be careful whom you choose. To find a qualified person, ask your veterinarian for a referral.

than just yelling at him to be quiet (which he won't understand until you teach him what it means) and then ignoring him when he is, give him an alternative to barking, and reward him for being quiet. Give him the *sit* or *down* command to distract him and give you control, and praise him when he's quiet. Make sure you're consistent—don't ignore his barking one time and yell at him the next. You'll probably never completely stop your Golden from barking, because it's natural for him to "speak" at times, but if you're patient, you should be able to prevent serious barkfests.

Some excessive barking is tied to other behavioral issues, such as separation anxiety, territoriality, or fear

due to lack of proper socialization. If that's the case, you need to work on the underlying cause before the barking will subside.

Chewing

Dogs love to chew, especially when they're young. Your puppy's deciduous (baby) teeth come in when he is about four weeks old. At four to five months old, his deciduous teeth loosen and fall out and are replaced by permanent (adult) teeth. While he's teething, he'll chew whatever he can grab to relieve the discomfort of swollen, painful gums. Some dogs enjoy chewing throughout their lives. It becomes a problem when your Golden chews the wrong things, but he wasn't born knowing what's legal mouth material and what isn't. You have to teach him.

Solution

Prevention is the best solution to problem chewing. Put anything you don't want your Golden to grab out of his reach. Then, teach your dog that he may chew some things but not everything. If he picks up something that he shouldn't, take it from him gently and replace it with one of his toys. Don't yell or punish him; teach him what's right. Be smart about the toys you give him, too. How is he supposed to know the difference between an old shoe you let him have and your brand-new ones? If he can't be trusted to choose his chewies wisely, then *never* leave him unsupervised in a situation where he can get to things he shouldn't have. Confine him to his crate with a nice chew toy or natural bone to play with when you can't watch him. Be consistent and think ahead, and your Golden will quickly learn what's allowed and what's off limits.

Digging

Some Golden Retrievers fancy themselves geologists, especially if they're bored, and most people don't like the results.

Solution

If your dog begins digging holes in your yard, you need to supervise his outdoor time until the pattern is broken, and you need to give him acceptable alternatives. As with other problem behaviors, simply seeing that your dog gets plenty of daily exercise may be all that's necessary to stop his excavations. Working on basic obedience, playing retrieving games, or getting involved in more advanced training in obedience, agility, tracking, or other sports are all good ways to redirect your Golden's energy.

If your Golden digs in one or two favorite spots, try filling or covering his hole with rocks, a heavy pot, or some other dig-proof barrier. Chicken wire buried horizontally under the top layer of soil will allow plants to grow while discouraging your dog from digging, and fencing or wire buried horizontally or vertically along a fence line will keep your dog from tunneling underneath.

If your Golden begins digging holes in your yard, supervise his outdoor time and give him some acceptable alternatives.

Certain substances can invite or discourage digging. Bonemeal or bloodmeal in a garden, for example, may entice your dog, who interprets the smells as buried animals. On the other hand, a variety of commercial and household products are said to be useful for stopping diggers, but many of them are only marginally effective, and some, like mothballs, are toxic. Besides, if your dog is digging due to boredom or excess energy, putting "stuff" in your yard won't give him an alternative behavior, and if he stops digging, he'll probably take up another hobby that you'll have to deal with.

Housetraining Problems

Inappropriate elimination—that is, pottying in the wrong places—is not a problem you want with a dog the size of a Golden Retriever. Fortunately, most Goldens are easy to housetrain, but problems do occasionally come up, especially with puppies and with older adoptees who lived in kennels or outdoors. Here are some suggestions about what you can do.

Solution

First, if your Golden is an adult or older puppy, and especially if he suddenly develops a potty problem, have your vet examine him to rule out a physical reason. Urinary tract infections, intestinal parasites, and other problems can rob your dog of control.

Once you've ruled out a health issue, you can move to training, or retraining. Regardless of your dog's age, follow the procedures outlined in Chapter 6. Until your dog is reliable, follow as regular a schedule as possible, and never leave your dog loose in the house unsupervised. If you're in the kitchen and your untrained dog urinates in the living room, it's not his fault, it's yours. Be sure that every member of the household understands this and follows the rules for as long as it takes to instill the new habit in your dog.

Jumping Up

Jumping up can be a big problem with a dog the size of a Golden Retriever, but it's important to understand that if your dog jumps on you, his goal isn't to dirty your clothes or knock you down. He jumps up because he likes you and he wants your attention. Chances are pretty good, too, that the people in his life have inadvertently rewarded him for jumping by getting excited and pushing him away, which he sees as play. He'll stop jumping up only when he realizes that it's not fun and not acceptable to you. The hardest part is

Jumping up can be problematic with a dog the size of a Golden Retriever.

making sure your family and friends don't reward the behavior and undermine your training.

Solution

One method that works if you're patient and consistent is to completely ignore your dog when he jumps up. (This method works very well for young puppies, but it is harder to stick to with a big, rough older puppy or an adult.) Fold your arms over your chest, turn your back on your dog, look up or away, and don't say a word. If he's been getting an interesting response from you in the past, your dog will keep trying for a while, but eventually he'll realize that jumping turns people into boring lumps rather than playmates, and he'll quit. When he does, talk to him calmly and pet him. If he jumps up again, become a lump.

To apply this approach effectively, you must plan ahead, be patient, and be absolutely consistent. If you ignore your jumping dog one time but reward him the next by getting excited, he'll keep jumping up in hopes that you'll "play." Don't wear good clothes around your dog until he's reliable; if necessary, get up a little earlier, take care of your dog, and then confine him before you get dressed for work. When you come home, change clothes before you let your dog out.

Another approach is to give your dog an alternative behavior. When you

When to Get Help With Aggression

Aggression, which includes serious growling, guarding, and biting, is absolutely unacceptable and abnormal behavior for a Golden Retriever. If your dog growls or bares his teeth, snaps, or guards his food, toys, bed, or other things, talk with his breeder, your veterinarian, or a qualified behaviorist. Sometimes a medical problem is to blame—abnormal hormone levels, for instance, can cause aggressive behavior, so schedule a thorough physical exam. Don't ignore aggression in the hope that it will get better on its own. It won't.

think he's about to jump up, tell him to do something else, like sit or lie down. When he does, praise him and give him a treat or other reward. Of course, your dog needs to understand the command you give, and if he doesn't yet understand it, you have to teach him as you go. That's fine, but yelling "SIT SIT SIT" as your dog leaps up won't teach him anything except that you're excitable.

There are a few things you should *not* do to teach your Golden to stay off you. Don't push him away or down, and don't follow the pushing down with petting. Being pushed or petted rewards him for jumping. Wait until he gets off on his own, and then pet him. Also, don't

FAMILY-FRIENDLY TIP

Supervising Child and Dog Interaction

Most Golden Retrievers are wonderful companions for kids, but no matter how much you trust your dog, all interaction between him and young children should be supervised by a responsible adult who can intervene immediately if necessary. Kid and dog interactions can get out of control very quickly, and both participants can end up frightened or injured or both.

Teach your child to respect your dog and to be kind and gentle with him. Kids aren't born knowing that it hurts to have eyes poked with fingers or hair pulled and twisted, and it's not fair to expect your Golden, no matter how long-suffering, to put up with abuse from a child. Similarly, teach your dog to be gentle and to keep his mouth off human flesh.

Golden Retrievers

knee, kick, or hit your dog for jumping up. Unless you're very coordinated, you probably won't connect, and if you do, you could injure your dog and teach him not to trust you. It's much more effective and fair to teach your dog that calm, polite behavior is what gets him what he wants.

Nipping and Mouthing

Golden Retrievers are born to carry things in their mouths, which can become a problem when your dog wants to carry human hands, arms, and other body parts. Although most Goldens have "soft" mouths—instinct tells them not to bite down on soft, fleshy things—your dog will frighten some people and seriously annoy others if he insists on "carrying" their limbs for them. And if he does accidentally squeeze too hard or bump someone's skin with a tooth, he could be in deep trouble for biting. If your Golden is still a puppy, he not only has the instinct to carry things, but like all puppies, he played with his siblings by using his mouth to bite, tug, grab, lick, and pull. He'll mouth people, too, until you teach him not to, and puppy teeth are sharp! So, pup or adult, your Golden needs to learn not to put his mouth and teeth on human skin, even in play. I'll suggest two methods I've found effective, but remember—it's very important for everyone who plays with or pets your dog to follow the "no mouthing" rule consistently.

Solution

One approach is to make mouthing counterproductive. Every time your pup puts his mouth on you, get up, walk away, and ignore him for a minute or so, and then return to what you were doing. If he pulls on your clothes or bites your ankles, leave the room for a minute and ignore him. Then come back and interact with him. As long as he doesn't grab you, he gets attention. If he uses his mouth, he gets ignored. Most dogs catch on very quickly to the new rules.

Another approach is to redirect your pup so that he has something "legal" in his mouth instead of flesh. This is especially effective between four and eight months or so when he's getting his permanent teeth and wants to chew all the time. If he mouths you, gently offer him a toy in place of your hand.

Like young children, tired puppies sometimes get cranky or silly and do a lot more mouthing than they do normally. If your pup has been awake and active for a while and his mouthing and other activity is out of control, he may need a nap. Put him in his crate and let him rest. He may whine for a minute or two and then fall asleep.

Never hit your Golden for mouthing or nipping (or anything else, for that matter). Hitting doesn't train your dog and nearly always causes more problems than you had to start with.

Unwanted behaviors can be frustrating. But if ever a breed of dog wanted to please people, it's the Golden Retriever. If you take the time to train your dog and look for the reasons behind your dog's mistakes, you will find the solutions to most of your problems. If you just can't get a handle on something, speak with your vet and look

SENIOR DOG TIP

Changing Old Habits

If you've adopted an older Golden Retriever, or if you've allowed your dog to develop a problem behavior, don't despair; most problems can be fixed. Here are some steps to take— the sooner the better:

- Make sure that your dog receives plenty of exercise—many problems are related to boredom.

- Be sure the problem isn't health related—schedule a checkup, and tell your vet about the behavior issue.

- Take your dog through a good basic obedience class. Many problems clear up when the dog is offered more structure and kind but firm rules for good behavior.

- Prevent your dog from behaving badly; if he's naughty when you can't supervise him, crate him.

- Break the pattern that promotes the behavior, and replace the unwanted old habit with an acceptable new habit.

for a good obedience class or qualified trainer or behaviorist. Be patient and keep at it, and most Goldens will become outstanding canine citizens.

93

In the Doghouse

Chapter 8

Stepping Out

Golden Retrievers are among the most versatile of dogs, and Goldens enjoy travel and excel in a variety of competitive sports and noncompetitive activities. In fact, training and participating in challenging activities is one of the most effective and fun ways to strengthen your relationship with your dog and channel his joy and exuberance. So let's get started!

Wherever You Go—Travel Tips

Golden Retrievers love to go where their people go, but they need to be protected when traveling.

Car Travel

Letting your dog ride loose in a car is risky, and he should never ride loose in the back of a truck. An unrestrained dog can be thrown around or out of the vehicle on turns and stops, and many dogs each year are injured or killed leaping or falling from windows or truck beds. Even letting your dog hang his head out the window is risky—dust and other debris hitting at the speed of a moving vehicle can seriously injure eyes and ears.

Your Golden rover is much safer traveling in a crate. If you're in an accident, the crate will protect him from injuries and keep him from escaping through an open door. If you're injured, someone will be able to see to your Golden's care more easily if he's confined. A doggy seatbelt is a reasonable alternative, although it won't protect him as well as a crate will. Air bags can injure or kill a dog, so don't strap your Golden into the front seat, no matter how much you enjoy having him beside you.

The heat in a parked car can kill your dog in just a few minutes even in relatively mild weather. If your dog can't get out of the car with you, leave him safe at home.

Never leave your Golden unattended in the car, even if the weather is mild.

Air Travel

Flying somewhere that you want to take your dog? Because of his size, your Golden will travel as cargo and must be in an airline-approved carrier with food and water containers and some sort of bedding. He'll need a health certificate issued by a veterinarian within ten days prior to the flight, and he should wear identification. Be sure to carry a leash with you. Different airlines have different policies, which are subject to change, and not all airlines transport animals, so check well in advance for booking requirements, prices, restrictions, and so on.

Accommodations

If you travel with your Golden, help keep pets welcome by obeying the rules of any accommodations where you stay or places you visit. Pick up your dog's waste and dispose of it properly—no one else wants to! Also, don't leave your dog alone to bark or cause problems. Keep your dog on a leash when outside, and don't let him rush up to other people or pets. It may be hard to believe, but some people don't appreciate a big, goofy dog.

Competitive Activities for Goldens

Golden Retrievers are among the most successful canine competitors, renowned for their intelligence, athletic abilities, and desire to please. If you

FAMILY-FRIENDLY TIP

Traveling With Dogs and Kids

A few extra precautions will make traveling with your dog and kids more pleasant and a lot safer for both. In addition to the general guidelines for safe travel, take a little time to help your child understand that care is necessary for your dog's safety. Be sure that any child who takes your dog out on leash has the strength needed to control the dog and the judgment needed to make good, sometimes quick, decisions. Teach your child never to open your dog's crate in the car (or to release a doggy seatbelt if you use one); the last thing you want is a loose dog at a rest stop. Teach your child not to feed the dog unauthorized treats while you're traveling. Finally, be a good role model by picking up after your dog and by putting your dog's safety and comfort before the lure of leaving him in a hot car or subjecting him to uncomfortable conditions such as crowds, hot sidewalks, or fireworks. Make trips fun—and safe—for everyone!

enjoy training your dog and like the thrill of competition, why not explore to agility only. The rules, procedures, obstacles, and jump heights differ from one to the next, so be sure to read the appropriate rule book before entering your dog in competition.

Conformation (Dog Showing)

Conformation shows are, in theory, designed to assess the quality of dogs who may at some time be used for breeding. The competition in Golden Retriever conformation is extremely tight, so your dog needs to be close to the perfection described by the breed standard to have any chance of winning. However, if you believe your dog is of that high caliber, you may want to give it a try. Your dog cannot be altered (spayed or neutered) to be shown in conformation, and you will need to learn how to groom and handle him properly for the show ring—it's not as easy as it looks on television! Many kennel clubs and training schools offer instruction on show handling, and your dog's breeder or other people who show Goldens may be willing to teach you to groom for the show ring.

If you purchased your Golden as a pet, not a show prospect, from a responsible breeder, please ask the breeder before you show the dog. Chances are you agreed to have the dog altered at a particular age, so that's one issue. Another is that serious breeders want only their best pups to be shown, because any dog in the ring

What to Pack for Your Roving Golden

- any medications your dog needs
- at least one toy (chewing is a good stress reliever)
- basic first-aid kit (see Chapter 5)
- bowls
- brush and nail clippers
- food
- identification
- leash(es)
- water

some dog sports? Win or lose, you'll come home with gold.

Agility

Golden Retrievers excel at agility, a sport in which the dog negotiates a timed course of jumps, tunnels, and other obstacles under his handler's direction.

The AKC, United Kennel Club (UKC), and ASCA (Australian Shepherd Club of America) offer agility programs in addition to their other competition programs. Two other organizations—the United States Dog Agility Association (USDAA) and the North American Dog Agility Council (NADAC)—are dedicated with the breeder's name on it reflects on the breeder's dogs and judgment. Your dog may have a fault that has no effect at all on his quality as a pet but makes him unsuited for the show ring. Your breeder trusted you with her puppy, so return the favor by trusting her judgment.

Field Training

Goldens were developed to retrieve shot birds for hunters, and there's nothing quite as thrilling as watching your dog's instinct kick in. The GRCA offers a noncompetitive Working Certificate program to test your Golden's ability and training to work as a hunting dog. The AKC offers a noncompetitive Hunt Test program, and the AKC and UKC both offer highly competitive trial programs.

Obedience

The sport of obedience demonstrates teamwork between the handler and dog, and Golden Retrievers consistently rank as top obedience competitors. In an obedience trial, the dog and handler perform a set of "exercises" that require specific commands from the handler and responses from the dog. The specific exercises vary according to the level of competition but may include heeling on and off leash, retrieving, finding things by scent, jumping, coming when called,

going to a specified place, and staying in a *sit* or a *down*.

If you're interested in trying this sport, find a qualified instructor, preferably one who has titled dogs in obedience and understands your personal goals, whether you just want to earn titles or you want to strive for big wins against tough competition.

Once you've trained and learned the rules, you'll be set to enter obedience trials, which are sanctioned by several organizations. The AKC obedience program offers obedience titles at all levels from novice through the elite National Obedience Champion. The Australian Shepherd Club of America (ASCA) and the United Kennel Club (UKC) also offer obedience titling programs for which Goldens are eligible.

In agility competition, a dog must negotiate a timed course of jumps, tunnels, and other obstacles.

What if Your Golden Isn't Registered?

If your Golden Retriever is not AKC registered but appears to be purebred and altered, you can apply for an Indefinite Listing Privilege (ILP) number. With an ILP, you and your dog can enter AKC events.

obedience trials, to earn a title. To earn a leg, he must score more than 50 percent on each exercise and have a total score of at least 170 out of 200 possible points.

One of the nice things about obedience competition is that you can set your own goals. If you're competitive and willing to put in lots of training time, you can aim for high scores, advanced titles, and other honors. If you aren't so competitive, you can aim for qualifying scores and obtain your dog's titles. Either way, you get to spend time with other people who love dogs, and best of all, with your Golden.

Rally Obedience

Rally obedience combines elements of competitive obedience and agility,

Each obedience program has its own rules and requirements, but in general, your dog must earn three legs, or qualifying scores in individual

Traveling with your Golden is a great way to strengthen your family's relationship with him.

requiring the handler and dog to negotiate a course with stations at which they demonstrate specific skills. Rally competition and titles have been available from the Association of Pet Dog Trainers (APDT) since 2001. The AKC rally obedience program began in January 2005, and both the UKC and ASCA are developing rally programs.

Tracking

Tracking—an activity in which a dog follows a scent trail—is a terrific way to channel energy. It's also awe-inspiring to watch your dog follow a line of scent that is completely outside your own sensory universe. You need to be reasonably fit physically to follow your dog as he tracks across hill and dale, and you need to have a fair amount of time to devote to training, but aside from that, you need little equipment (a harness and long line, flags to mark the track initially, small articles for your dog to find, a notebook and pen to map your tracks, and food for rewarding your dog).

Your Golden can even earn tracking titles at tracking tests, which evaluate your dog's ability to recognize and follow human scent. Tracking is great fun.

Noncompetitive Activities for Goldens

Golden Retrievers are among the sweetest dogs going, but they also have lots of energy, especially when they're young. You'll enjoy your dog

Keep Canine Sports Safe

When starting a new activity, start modestly and work up slowly. This is especially important for a growing puppy (up to about 18 months); young bones and joints are easily injured, and injury can last a lifetime. Be particularly cautious about jumping or running your dog on hard surfaces. Keep your dog in proper weight and condition, warm him up before each performance, and don't ask him to do anything for which he isn't properly trained.

more (and vice versa) if you direct his physical and mental energy into safe, fun activities. Let's look at a few you might like.

Walking, Jogging, and Hiking

Goldens are wonderful walking, jogging, or hiking partners. You don't need much equipment for these activities, and they'll help keep you both in shape. But there are some hazards involved, so take a few simple precautions before you head out the door.

Exercise Preparations

Start your exercise program slowly and build up. If you or your dog hasn't had a checkup lately, it would be a good idea to get one. Ask your doctor and

101

vet about a safe exercise program and diet if either of you is overweight. Be sure your dog's vaccinations are current, and if you're traveling or going into wild areas, ask your vet whether your dog needs protection from any diseases that don't pose a threat at home. Use a heartworm preventive and an effective tick control as needed for the area. Also, take care of your Golden's feet (see Chapter 4), and check them for cuts or scrapes before, during, and after your outing. Check him also for burrs and other debris that may be caught in his coat.

Even a well-trained Golden can be a handful, so be sure that whoever takes your dog out can control him under all circumstances. If your child wants to walk your dog, a responsible adult should be present in case of emergency. What would your child do, for instance, if another dog attacked yours during a walk?

Equipment

Your dog needs a collar that fits well and is in good condition, with his identification tag or tags, rabies tag, and license tag attached to it. He also needs a leash, which can be the difference between life and death for your dog, and which will keep him from disturbing other people, pets, and wildlife. A retractable leash is good in some situations but can be a tangled nuisance in the woods, and many parks require dogs to be on leashes 6 feet (1.8 m) or shorter. Check your leash frequently for wear, especially around the bolt—a broken leash far from home is no fun. Most leashes have a loop at the end, but slipping your hand through the loop may not be a great idea. I have seen a wrist get broken by a sudden lunge of a dog much smaller than the average Golden. Teach children never to slide

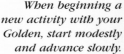

When beginning a new activity with your Golden, start modestly and advance slowly.

their hands through the loop or put a leash around any part of their bodies, particularly their neck. And don't let your dog off leash in unfenced areas—it takes only one small mistake for tragic consequences to result.

Exercise Precautions

In hot weather, keep outings short and avoid the hottest part of the day. The sun can make paved surfaces painfully hot for your dog to walk on, and the heat reflected from hot surfaces can raise his body temperature to dangerous levels. Be sure your dog has frequent access to clean, cool water when exercising in hot weather. Goldens tolerate cold weather well, but extreme low temperatures can cause hypothermia or frostbite, so be alert to signs, such as shivering, that indicate that your dog is getting cold if he's out for a long time. Avoid walking where chemicals have been used, and if you can't avoid them, wash your dog's feet with warm water and dog shampoo to remove toxic substances.

Waste pickup isn't the greatest job in the world, but leaving your dog's waste for someone else to pick up—or step in—is beyond rude. Pick up after your dog, and deposit it in a proper receptacle (at home, if necessary).

Be sure that dogs are allowed where you plan to go—many parks and natural areas prohibit dogs. Those that allow dogs usually require leashes at all times. Good trail etiquette will go a

SENIOR DOG TIP

Traveling With Your Golden Oldie

If your Golden is entering his senior years (seven or older), be sensitive to his reactions to leaving home. If he seems confused, agitated, or nervous or refuses to eat, drink, or eliminate normally, consider leaving him home next time. He's probably a lot happier there. But if he seems happy and healthy, by all means take him along!

long way toward making sure dogs remain welcome in parks and on trails, so teach your Golden to sit or lie quietly beside the path to let other people pass.

If you plan to be out for several hours, don't forget water. Bring a small bowl (collapsible pet bowls are available from many pet supply stores) or teach your dog to drink from a squirt bottle. Try not to let your dog drink from water sources along the way—they may be contaminated with bacteria and chemicals. Have a wonderful time with your Golden friend!

The Canine Good Citizen test rewards well-trained dogs and their owners.

The Golden Good Citizen

Once your Golden has mastered the basics of polite behavior, he can take the American Kennel Club (AKC) Canine Good Citizen (CGC) test, which is frequently offered by dog clubs and others as a way of promoting responsible dog ownership and rewarding well-trained dogs and their owners.

The CGC test is made up of ten subtests that determine that your dog is well cared for, has basic obedience skills, is under control, and is polite around strange people and dogs. To take the CGC test, you must present proof of rabies vaccination and provide your dog's own brush or comb. Your dog must wear a buckle or slip (choke) collar made of leather, fabric, or chain, and he must be on leash throughout the test.

Calling Doctor Golden

If you enjoy volunteering, you and your Golden might find animal-assisted activities (AAA) or animal-assisted therapy (AAT) rewarding. AAA includes visits to people in nursing homes, literacy and reading programs, hospitals, schools, and other environments without the participation of a professional health worker or formal records of the dog's effect on the people he visits. AAT, in contrast, is an activity in which an animal and handler work with a professional therapist, teacher, or doctor who directs their activities and keeps records to assess the benefits of the visits in some systematic way. Many Golden Retrievers participate in AAT and AAA programs, and several organizations certify dogs as suitable for AAA and AAT activities. The term "therapy dog"

is often used to indicate a dog who participates in AAA or AAT.

Therapy dogs should not be confused with "service dogs," who work as guide dogs for the blind, hearing dogs for the deaf, seizure alert dogs, general assistance dogs, and so on. Therapy dogs do not need the specialized training that service dogs receive and do not have the legal rights afforded to service dogs under the Americans with Disabilities Act (ADA).

Whatever activities you choose to take up with your Golden, and however successful you might be, remember always that the real prizes to be won are your dog's love, respect, and companionship.

Some Golden Retrievers function as service dogs.

Resources

Associations and Organizations

Registries and Breed Clubs

American Kennel Club (AKC)
5580 Centerview Drive
Raleigh, NC 27606
Telephone: (919) 233-9767
Fax: (919) 233-3627
E-mail: info@akc.org
www.akc.org

Canadian Kennel Club (CKC)
89 Skyway Avenue, Suite 100
Etobicoke, Ontario M9W 6R4
Telephone: (416) 675-5511
Fax: (416) 675-6506
E-mail: information@ckc.ca
www.ckc.ca

Federation Cynologique Internationale (FCI)
Secretariat General de la FCI
Place Albert 1er, 13
B – 6530 Thuin
Belqique
www.fci.be

The Golden Retriever Club of America
www.grca.org

The Kennel Club
1 Clarges Street
London
W1J 8AB
Telephone: 0870 606 6750
Fax: 0207 518 1058
www.the-kennel-club.org.uk

United Kennel Club (UKC)
100 E. Kilgore Road
Kalamazoo, MI 49002-5584
Telephone: (269) 343-9020
Fax: (269) 343-7037
E-mail: pbickell@ukcdogs.com
www.ukcdogs.com

Pet Sitters

National Association of Professional Pet Sitters
15000 Commerce Parkway, Suite C
Mt. Laurel, New Jersey 08054
Telephone: (856) 439-0324
Fax: (856) 439-0525
E-mail: napps@ahint.com
www.petsitters.org

Pet Sitters International
201 East King Street
King, NC 27021-9161
Telephone: (336) 983-9222
Fax: (336) 983-5266
E-mail: info@petsit.com
www.petsit.com

Rescue Organizations and Animal Welfare Groups

American Humane Association (AHA)
63 Inverness Drive East
Englewood, CO 80112
Telephone: (303) 792-9900
Fax: 792-5333
www.americanhumane.org

American Society for the Prevention of Cruelty to Animals (ASPCA)
424 E. 92nd Street
New York, NY 10128-6804
Telephone: (212) 876-7700
www.aspca.org

Royal Society for the Prevention of Cruelty to Animals (RSPCA)
Telephone: 0870 3335 999
Fax: 0870 7530 284
www.rspca.org.uk

The Humane Society of
the United States (HSUS)
2100 L Street, NW
Washington DC 20037
Telephone: (202) 452-1100
www.hsus.org

Sports

International Agility Link (IAL)
Global Administrator: Steve Drinkwater
E-mail: yunde@powerup.au
www.agilityclick.com/~ial

North American Flyball Association
www.flyball.org
1400 West Devon Avenue #512
Chicago, IL 6066
800-318-6312

World Canine Freestyle Organization
P.O. Box 350122
Brooklyn, NY 11235-2525
Telephone: (718) 332-8336
www.worldcaninefreestyle.org

Therapy

Delta Society
875 124th Ave NE, Suite 101
Bellevue, WA 98005
Telephone: (425) 226-7357
Fax: (425) 235-1076
E-mail: info@deltasociety.org
www.deltasociety.org

Therapy Dogs Incorporated
PO Box 5868
Cheyenne, WY 82003
Telephone: (877) 843-7364
E-mail: therdog@sisna.com
www.therapydogs.com

Therapy Dogs International (TDI)
88 Bartley Road
Flanders, NJ 07836
Telephone: (973) 252-9800
Fax: (973) 252-7171
E-mail: tdi@gti.net
www.tdi-dog.org

Training

Association of Pet Dog Trainers (APDT)
150 Executive Center Drive Box 35
Greenville, SC 29615
Telephone: (800) PET-DOGS
Fax: (864) 331-0767
E-mail: information@apdt.com
www.apdt.com

National Association of Dog Obedience Instructors (NADOI)
PMB 369
729 Grapevine Hwy.
Hurst, TX 76054-2085
www.nadoi.org

Veterinary and Health Resources

American Animal Hospital Association (AAHA)
P.O. Box 150899
Denver, CO 80215-0899
Telephone: (303) 986-2800
Fax: (303) 986-1700
E-mail: info@aahanet.org
www.aahanet.org/index.cfm

American Holistic Veterinary Medical Association (AHVMA)
2218 Old Emmorton Road
Bel Air, MD 21015
Telephone: (410) 569-0795
Fax: (410) 569-2346
E-mail: office@ahvma.org
www.ahvma.org

American Veterinary Medical Association (AVMA)
1931 North Meacham Road – Suite 100
Schaumburg, IL 60173
Telephone: (847) 925-8070
Fax: (847) 925-1329
E-mail: avmainfo@avma.org
www.avma.org

ASPCA Animal Poison Control Center
1717 South Philo Road, Suite 36
Urbana, IL 61802
Telephone: (888) 426-4435
www.aspca.org

British Veterinary Association (BVA)
7 Mansfield Street
London
W1G 9NQ
Telephone: 020 7636 6541
Fax: 020 7436 2970
E-mail: bvahq@bva.co.uk
www.bva.co.uk

Publications

Books

Adamson, Eve. *The Golden Retriever*. Neptune City:TFH Publications, 2005.

Anderson,Teoti. *The Super Simple Guide to Housetraining*. Neptune City:TFH Publications, 2004.

Boneham, Sheila Webster, Ph.D. *The Complete Idiot's Guide to Getting and Owning a Dog*. Alpha Books, 2002.

Morgan, Diane. *Good Dogkeeping*. Neptune City:TFH Publications, 2005.

Yin, Sophia, DVM. *How to Behave So Your Dog Behaves*. Neptune City:TFH Publications, 2004.

Magazines

AKC Family Dog
American Kennel Club
260 Madison Avenue
New York, NY 10016
Telephone: (800) 490-5675
E-mail: familydog@akc.org
www.akc.org/pubs/familydog

AKC Gazette
American Kennel Club
260 Madison Avenue
New York, NY 10016
Telephone: (800) 533-7323
E-mail: gazette@akc.org
www.akc.org/pubs/gazette

Dog & Kennel
Pet Publishing, Inc.
7-L Dundas Circle
Greensboro, NC 27407
Telephone: (336) 292-4272
Fax: (336) 292-4272
E-mail: info@petpublishing.com
www.dogandkennel.com

Dog Fancy
Subscription Department
P.O. Box 53264
Boulder, CO 80322-3264
Telephone: (800) 365-4421
E-mail: barkback@dogfancy.com
www.dogfancy.com

Dogs Monthly
Ascot House
High Street,Ascot,
Berkshire SL5 7JG
United Kingdom
Telephone: 0870 730 8433
Fax: 0870 730 8431
E-mail: admin@rtc-associates.freeserve.co.uk
www.corsini.co.uk/dogsmonthly

Index

Note: Boldface numbers indicate illustrations; an italic *t* indicates a table.

A

accommodations during travel, 97
acupuncture, 68
adopting the older dog, 21
adult dogs
  adoption of, 21
  feeding, 30*t*
aggression, 91
agility competition, 98
air travel, 97
allergies, 27, 65
alternative therapies, 67–68
American Academy of Veterinary Acupuncture (AAVA), 68
American Holistic Veterinary Medical Association (AHVMA), 69
American Kennel Club (AKC), 98, 99, 104
Americans with Disabilities Act (ADA), 105
amount to feed, age-specific, 29–33
anal sac care, 46–47
animal-assisted activities (AAA), 105
animal-assisted therapy (AAT), 105
artificial ingredients in foods, 25
Association of Pet Dog Trainers (APDT), 101
Australian Shepherd Club of America (ASCA), 98, 99

B

baby gates, 14
barking, 86–88
bathing your Golden Retriever, 39–41, **41**, **42**
beds and bedding, 14–15
begging, 35
behaviorists, 88
bite wounds, 66
biting, 92–93
bleeding, 66
body, 8

bones and joints, 64–65
  elbow dysplasia in, 65
  fractures in, 66, **66**
  hip dysplasia (CHD) in, 64–65
  hip dysplasia and, 62
bones in diet, 28–29
bordetellosis (kennel cough), 53
bowls for food and water, 17
brushes and brushing, 38–39, **39**

C

calcium, 26
cancer, 61
canine behaviorists, 88
Canine Good Citizen (CGC) program, 104–105
canned foods, 26
car travel, 96, **96**
cataracts of the eye, 45, 62–63
celebrity owners of Golden Retrievers, 7
central progressive retinal atrophy (CPRA) and, 63
chew toys and dental health, 46
chewing, 88–89
children and the Golden Retriever, 10, 19, 25, 43, 51, 79, 92, 97
choke chains, 72–73
city home for Golden Retrievers, 11
coat and skin, 6–7. *See also* grooming
  allergies and, 27, 65
  hot spots in, 65
  mange and mites in, 56
  ringworm in, 59
collars, 15, 72–73, 102–103
color, 6–7
colostrum and immune function in puppies, 51
come command, 78–80
commercial dog foods, 24–27
communicating with your Golden Retriever, 75
complementary medical therapies, 67–68
conformation showing, 98–99
crate training, 74
crate, **14**, 15–16, 74
cuts, 66

D

daycare for dogs, 16

dental care, 45–46, **46**
  brushing your dog's teeth in, 46
  chew toys and, 46
digging, 89–90
distemper, 52–53
dog foods, 24–27
dog shows, 98–99
dog walkers, 16
doggie daycare, 16
down command, 81, **80**
dry food or kibble, 25–26
dysplasia, 64–65

E

ears and ear care, 7, 43–44, 61–62, **61**
elbow dysplasia, 65
emergency medical care, 65–67
endocrine system problems, 62
entropion/ectropion, 63
environment for the Golden Retriever, 11
epilepsy and seizures, 64
exercise pens (x-pens), 16–17, **17**
exercise programs, 101–103
exercise requirements, 9–11
eyes and eye care, 7, 44–45, 62–63
  cataracts of the eye in, 45, 62–63
  central progressive retinal atrophy (CPRA) and, 63
  entropion/ectropion in, 63
  infections in, 45
  nuclear sclerosis of the eye and, 45
  retinal dysplasia and, 63
  trichiasis/distichiasis in, 63

F

feeding, 23–35
  adult dogs, 30*t*
  allergies and, 27, 65
  amount to feed in, age-specific, 29–33
  artificial ingredients in, 25
  bones in, 28–29
  bowls for, 17
  canned foods in, 26
  commercial diets in, 24–27
  dry food or kibble in, 25–26
  home-cooked foods in, 28
  noncommercial diets and, 27–29
  obesity and, 33–35

price vs. quality of foods in, 24–25
puppies, 30*t*
raw food diets (BARF diet) in, 28–29
schedule for, 29–33
semi-moist foods in, 26
senior dogs, 30*t*, 31
special-formula foods in, 26–27
supplements and, 26
table manners and, 35
treats and, 28
water requirements and, 30
feet, 41–43
field training, 99
first aid, 65–67
first-aid kit, 69
fleas and flea control, 55–56
Food and Drug Administration (FDA), herbal therapy and, 69
fractures, 66, **66**
friendliness, 11

G

gait, 8
gates, 14
giardia infection, 58
Golden Retriever Club of America (GRCA), 61
grooming, 11, 37–47
anal sac care in, 46–47
bathing in, 39–41, **41**, **42**
brushes and brushing in, 38–39, **39**
dental care and, 45–46, **46**
ear care in, 43–44
eye care in, 44–45
health check during, 40
nail care in, 41–43, **44**
senior dogs and, 47
supplies for, 18–19, 38
tables for, 42
grooming tables, 42
guide dogs, 105

H

halters (head collars), 73
head, 7
health issues, 49–69
acupuncture in, 68
allergies and, 27, 65
alternative therapies in, 67–68
anal sac impaction and, 46–47
bordetellosis (kennel cough) in, 53
calcium and, 26
cancer and, 61
cataracts of the eye in, 45, 62–63
central progressive retinal atrophy (CPRA) and, 63
cuts, bites, bleeding in, 66
dental care and, 45–46, **46**
distemper in, 52–53
ears and ear care in, 61–62, **61**
elbow dysplasia in, 65
endocrine system problems and, 62
epilepsy and seizures in, 64
exercise programs and, 101–103
eyes and eye care in, 44–45, 62–63
first aid in, 65–67
first-aid kit for, 69
fleas and flea control in, 55–56
fractures in, 66, **66**
giardia infection in, 58
grooming and, as check for, 40
heart disease in, 63–64
heartworm in, 58–59
heatstroke in, 66–67, 103
hepatitis in, 54
herbal medicine in, 68–69
hip dysplasia (CHD) in, 62, 64
homeopathy and, 69
hookworm in, 58
housesoiling and, 90
hypervitaminosis and, 26
hypothyroidism and, 62
insurance for, 53
leptospirosis in, 53
life span, 9
mange and mites in, 56
neurological problems in, 64
nuclear sclerosis of the eye and, 45
obesity and, 33–35
orthopedic problems in, 64–65
parainfluenza in, 53
parasites in, 55–57
parvovirus (CPV) in, 53–54
poisons in, 67
rabies in, 54–55
retinal dysplasia and, 63
ringworm in, 59
roundworm in, 59–60
safety and sports in, 101
senior dogs and, 67
skin problems in, 65
spaying and neutering (altering) in, 50–51
special-formula foods and, 26–27
subvalvular aortic stenosis (SAS) in, 63–64
supplements and, 26
tapeworm in, 60
ticks and tick removal in, 56–57
vaccinations in, 51–55
veterinarian selection and vet visits in, 50
vitamin and mineral supplements and, 26
whipworms in, 60
worms and worming in, 57–58
heart disease, 63–64
heartworm, 58–59
heatstroke, 66–67, 103
hepatitis, 54
herbal medicine, 68–69
hiking with your Golden Retriever, 101–103
hip dysplasia (CHD), 62, 64
holistic medicine, 67–68
home-cooked foods, 28
homeopathy, 69
hookworm, 58
hot spots, 65
hot weather precautions, 103. *See also* heatstroke
housesoiling, 90
housetraining, 9, 74–77, 90
accidents in, 75–76
Hunt Test, 99
hypervitaminosis, 26
hypothyroidism, 62

I

identification, 19
insurance, health/medical, 53
internal parasites. *See* worms and worming

J

jogging with your Golden Retriever, 101–103
jumping up, 90–92, **90**

K

kennel cough, 53
kibble, 25–26

L

leashes, 19–20, 73, 102–103

leave it command, 82-83, 82
leptospirosis, 53
licensing your Golden
    Retriever, 18
life span, 9
lost dogs, 87

M
mange and mites in, 56
medical/health insurance, 53
microchipping, 19
mites and mange, 56
motels/hotels, 97

N
nail care, 41-43, **44**
neurological problems, 64
nipping and mouthing, 92-93
North American Dog Agility
    Council (NADAC), 98
nuclear sclerosis of the eye, 45

O
obedience competition,
    99-100
obesity, 33-35
Orthopedic Foundation for
    Animals (OFA), 62
orthopedic problems, 64-65

P
parainfluenza, 53
parasites, 55-57
parvovirus (CPV), 53-54
personality, 6, 8-9, 11
Poison Control Hotline num-
    bers, 69
poisons, 67
positive reinforcement train-
    ing, 72
problem behaviors, 85-93
    aggression as, 91
    barking as, 86-88
    begging as, 35
    canine behaviorists to help
        with, 88
    chewing as, 88-89
    digging as, 89-90
    housesoiling as, 90
    jumping up as, 90-92, **90**
    nipping and mouthing as,
        92-93
    senior dogs and, 93
professional obedience instruc-
    tors/trainers, 77
puppies
    adult dog adoption vs., 21
    colostrum and immune
        function in, 51
    feeding, 30*t*

housetraining and, 9, 74-77
nipping and mouthing in,
    92-93
socialization in, 73-74
spaying and neutering
    (altering) in, 50-51
vaccinations and, 51-55

Q
quality of foods, 24-25

R
rabies, 54-55
rally obedience, 100-101
raw food diets (BARF diet),
    28-29
registering your Golden
    Retriever, 100
retinal dysplasia, 63
ringworm, 59
roundworm, 59-60
rural home for Golden
    Retrievers, 11

S
safety and sports, 101
schedule for your Golden
    Retriever, 15
scheduled feedings, 29-33
search-and-rescue dogs, 11
seizures, 64
semi-moist foods, 26
senior dogs, 9
    adoption of, 21
    feeding, 30*t*, 31
    grooming of, 47
    health care for, 67
    problem behaviors in, 93
    training, 81
    traveling with, 103
service dogs, 11, 105, **105**
showing your Golden
    Retriever, 98-99
sit command, 77-78, **78**
size and weight, 6
skin. *See* coat and skin
socialization, 73-74
spaying and neutering (alter-
    ing), 50-51
special-formula foods, 26-27
stay command, 80-81
subvalvular aortic stenosis
    (SAS), 63-64
supplements, 26

T
table manners, 35
tapeworm, 60
tattoos for identification, 19
teeth, 7-8. *See also* dental care

therapy dogs, 105
ticks and tick removal, 56-57
toys and chewies, 20-21, 73
tracking competition, 101
training, 71-83
    collars and choke chains in,
        72-73
    come command in, 78-80
    communicating with your
        Golden Retriever in, 75
    crate, 74
    down command in, 81, **80**
    housetraining and, 9, 74-77,
        90
    leashes in, 73
    leave it command in, 82-83
    positive reinforcement in,
        72
    problem behaviors and. *See*
        problem behaviors
    professional obedience
        instructors/trainers for,
        77
    senior dogs and, 81
    sit command in, 77-78, **78**
    socialization in, 73-74
    stay command in, 80-81
    table manners, 35
    treats and toys used in, 73
    walking nicely on a leash
        and, 81-82
traveling with your Golden
    Retriever, 96-97, 98, 103
treats, 28, 73
trichiasis/distichiasis, 63

U
United Kennel Club (UKC), 98,
    99
United States Dog Agility
    Association (USDAA), 98

V
veterinarian selection and vet
    visits, 50
vitamin and mineral supple-
    ments, 26

W
walking with your Golden
    Retriever, 81-82, 101-103
water requirements and, 30
whipworms, 60
worms and worming, 57-58

X
x-pens (exercise pens), 16-17,
    17

111

Index

Dedication

For Clancy and Ruby—you may lie on my couch any time you like.

About the Author

Sheila Webster Boneham, Ph.D., loves dogs and writing about dogs. Three of her books have won the prestigious Maxwell Award from the Dog Writers Association of America, including *The Simple Guide to Labrador Retrievers*, named Best Single Breed Book of 2002. For the past decade, Sheila has taught people about dogs through her writing and other activities. She hopes that her successes and mistakes as a puppy buyer, breeder, trainer, owner, and rescuer can benefit other dog lovers and their dogs. Sheila and her canine companions are active in competition and in dog-assisted activities and therapy. A former university writing teacher, Sheila also conducts writing workshops. You can visit Sheila and her dogs on the web at www.sheilaboneham.com.

Photo Credits